Baptism Now Saves You

Baptism Now Saves You

How Water & Spirit Give Eternal Life

Karlo Broussard

Catholic Answers Press

Published by Catholic Answers, Inc.
2020 Gillespie Way
El Cajon, California 92020
1-888-291-8000 orders
619-387-0042 fax
catholic.com

Printed in the United States of America

Cover design by Theodore Schluenderfritz
Interior design by Nora Malone

978-1-68357-396-8
978-1-68357-397-5 Kindle
978-1-68357-398-2 ePub

To all born-again Christians

Contents

Introduction

In Matthew 28:19, Jesus told his apostles, "Go therefore and make disciples of all nations, *baptizing* them in the name of the Father and of the Son and of the Holy Spirit." Clearly, baptism is something that's important to Jesus. He makes it part of the initial phase of becoming a believer.

But what *precisely* did Christ intend the nature of baptism to be?

Some Christians say it's *merely* a visible expression of a Christian's *salvation* in Jesus, which comes about through faith.[1] Others, including Catholics, say that baptism indeed does symbolize a person's belief in Jesus, but it *also* brings about an inner renewal—a rebirth—that makes the baptized person a child of God. Such a renewal, on this view, consists of the baptized going from a state of unrighteousness (lacking a right relationship with God—i.e., not being justified) to a state of righteousness (having a right relationship with God—i.e., being justified). Christians call this interior change "regeneration."

The vast majority of Christians believe that baptism is a cause of salvation, including Catholics, Eastern Orthodox, Oriental Orthodox, Lutherans, Anglicans, Methodists, and even some Calvinists. Only Baptists and those springing from the radical side of the Reformation reject this.

Which of the above views is correct? And even if we can settle this question, we still need to know *how* a person should be baptized. Should a person be baptized with the words "in the name of the Father, the Son, and the Holy Spirit," or should the words "in the name of Christ" or "Jesus" be used? Should a person be fully immersed in water, or is pouring or sprinkling sufficient?

The purpose of this book is to answer these questions, along with many more, and provide a clear and concise explanation and defense of the full Catholic teaching on baptism in the face of differing interpretations.

The book is divided into four parts.

The first part deals with the *evidence* that baptism saves. In the first three chapters, we appeal to Jesus, St. Paul, and St. Peter, defending passages in the New Testament that, Catholics believe, teach baptismal regeneration. In chapters four and five, we survey early Christian testimony (from the first to the fourth century) on the salvific efficacy of baptism and magisterial teaching in the Catholic Church from the fifth century on.

The second part of the book, chapters six through nine, addresses certain questions that arise concerning the *practice* of baptism. Among them,

- Who is the minister of the sacrament? Is it the priest only? Or can anyone baptize?
- Who can receive the sacrament? Is the sacrament only for adults, or can infants be baptized, too?
- What's the proper mode of baptism? Can we pour, or must we immerse?
- Is the trinitarian formula valid, or must we use the "in the name of Jesus" formula, like what we see in the Bible?

Part three shifts from the apologetical arena to the arena of theology proper. In chapter ten, we address questions that arise due to the relation between baptism and salvation. For example, what's the scope of the renewal that baptism brings about within us? Is it limited to just original sin, or does it involve personal sins as well? Also, does baptism remit anything else that may be related to sin?

The most important question that weighs heavy on the hearts and minds of folks within this chapter is whether someone who dies without baptism, whether an adult or a child, still goes to heaven.

Chapter eleven takes up questions that pertain to the relationship between baptism and faith. As we'll see, faith is necessary for baptism. But if that's the case, why get baptized? To be able to have faith before baptism seems to make baptism superfluous and not salvific.

Chapter twelve deals with the topic of the sacramental seal. What is this seal? What does it do? Can we lose it as baptized Christians? We answer these questions and more to shed light on this mystery.

The last part of the book, part four, focuses on the *life* of the baptized. The idea here is that people want to know, "What are the implications for my life once I'm baptized?" We highlight two aspects of the life of the baptized:

1. the implications for our lives as Christians and
2. the significance of our relationship with the Church.

I pray that this book will help you better appreciate the mystery of this "gateway to life in the Spirit" (*Catechism of the Catholic Church* [CCC] 1213) and be inspired to give thanks to God for the gift of *new* life that's given in the *new* birth of baptism.

Part 1

The Evidence

Chapter 1

Jesus Says So

When it comes to biblical support for the belief in baptismal regeneration, there's no better place to start than with Jesus himself. John 3:3–5, commonly known as the "Born Again" discourse, is *the* key passage for Jesus' revelation of baptismal regeneration. Here's the text:

> "Truly, truly, I say to you, unless one is born anew, he cannot see the kingdom of God." Nicodemus said to him, "How can a man be born when he is old? Can he enter a second time into his mother's womb and be born?" Jesus answered, "Truly, truly, I say to you, unless one is born of *water and the Spirit*, he cannot enter the kingdom of God."

The Council of Trent appealed to this passage in its teaching that natural water is necessary for baptism, stating in Canon 2 of its Canons on the Sacrament of Baptism, "If any one shall say, that true and natural water is not of necessity for baptism, and, on that account, wrests to some sort of metaphor those words of our Lord Jesus Christ, *Except a man be born again of water and them Holy Ghost*, let him be anathema."[2]

A Positive Exegesis

Jesus' above statement comes within the context of a conversation that Jesus has with Nicodemus, "a teacher of Israel" (v.10). Jesus had told Nicodemus that to enter the kingdom of God, one must be "born anew" (v.3), which prompted a question: "How can a man be born when he is old? Can he enter a second time into his mother's womb and be born?" (v.4). It's in response to this question by Nicodemus that Jesus says, "Unless one is born of water and the Spirit, he cannot enter the kingdom of God" (v.5).

What do water and spirit refer to? We say baptism. But why?

There are two arguments we can give here to defend this claim. The first is derived from Jesus' implication that what he's talking about is rooted in the Jewish scriptures.

After revealing that a person must be born again to enter God's kingdom, Jesus tells Nicodemus, "Do not marvel that I said to you, 'You must be born anew'" (v.7). This prompts Nicodemus to ask again, "How can this be?" (v.9). Jesus answers, "Are you a teacher of Israel, and yet you do not understand this?" (v.10).

The implication here is that Jesus' teaching about water, spirit, and new birth is rooted in Jewish tradition. And since Nicodemus is a teacher of that tradition, he should know about it.

But where in Jewish tradition? The answer is Ezekiel 36:25-27:

> I will sprinkle clean water upon you, and you shall be clean from all your uncleannesses, and from all your idols I will cleanse you. A new heart I will give you, and a new spirit I will put within you; and I will take out of your flesh the heart of stone and give you a heart of flesh. And I will put my spirit within you, and cause you to walk in my statutes and be careful to observe my ordinances.

Notice how this passage contains the same themes present in Jesus' conversation with Nicodemus: water, God's spirit, and renewal. Given the combination of these themes, this is likely what Jesus expects Nicodemus to think of when he speaks of a *new* birth by *water* and *Spirit*. Jesus is teaching Nicodemus that the rebirth by water and Spirit *is* the event of cleansing and renewal that Ezekiel prophesied.

But what is this rebirth by water and Spirit, precisely? The answer is baptism. First-century Jews associated the hope of the age, when God would cleanse and renew his people by water and Spirit found in Ezekiel's prophecy, with a baptismal ministry. The *Jewish Encyclopedia* says of this time,

> To receive the spirit of God, or to be permitted to stand in the presence of God (his *Shekinah*), man must undergo baptism ... in the messianic time God will himself pour water of purification upon Israel in accordance with Ezekiel 36:25.[3]

The late New Testament scholar George Beasley-Murray explains,

> The conjunction of water and Spirit in eschatological hope is deeply rooted in the Jewish consciousness, as is attested by Ezekiel 36:25-27 and various apocalyptic writings (e.g., *Jub.* 1:23; *Pss. Sol.* 18:6; Test *Jud* 24:3), but above all the literature and practices of the Qumran sectaries, who sought to unite cleansing and the hope of the Spirit *with actual immersions* and repentance in a community beginning to "see" the kingdom of God (cf. 1QS 3:6-9; 1QH 11:12-14).[4]

If the Jews saw the event of Ezekiel's prophecy as a baptism for the age of cleansing and renewal, and Jesus intends Nicodemus to understand rebirth by water and Spirit in terms of that event, then it follows that Jesus intends baptism to be the new birth by water and Spirit.

This interpretation that the new birth refers to baptism is further confirmed by the preceding and subsequent context of the passage in question, which makes for a second argument in favor of the sacramental interpretation of the text. The images of Spirit and water *together* constitute the one event of Jesus' baptism, which John hints at in John 1:29-34. In John 3:23, he records how John the Baptist was baptizing at Aenon near Salim. We're also told in John 4:1-2 that the apostles went about baptizing.

If the instruction to be born again of water and Spirit is surrounded both before and after by the theme of baptism, then it's reasonable to conclude that baptism is what Jesus has in mind when he speaks of the necessity to be born of water and spirit for entrance into heaven. And if that's the case, then Jesus reveals that baptism saves.

Counterarguments

Not all Christians interpret the new birth in John 3:3-5 as a reference to baptism. This is so for a variety of reasons.

"Water" Is a Symbol for the Holy Spirit

Some Christians arrive at different conclusions about what it means to be "born of water." Take, for example, Protestant pastor Todd Baker, who pastors Shalom Messianic Congregation in Dallas, Texas, and is the president of Brit-Hadashah Ministries. In volume one of his book *Exodus from Rome*, he argues that the "water" spoken of in John 3:3-5 is merely a symbol for the Holy Spirit. For evidence, he appeals to the very prophecy quoted above: Ezekiel 36:25-27. He writes,

> God was going to pour out his Spirit upon all Israel, so that the nation would be renewed, purified, and washed from sin by the cleansing powers of the Holy Spirit, *just*

> *as water removes dirt and filth*. . . . [This passage] connect[s] the metaphor of water with the Spirit together in the acts of sprinkling and pouring out to convey the combined work of cleansing from impurity and renewal from spiritual death that will occur when God's Spirit is poured out like clean and living water. . . .
>
> Rome's faulty interpretation that water baptism is meant in John 3:5 is nothing more than a clever inference from the word "water," which apparently ignores how the symbol for water, representing the Holy Spirit, is repeatedly employed throughout both the Old and New Testaments of the Bible.[5]

One problem with Baker's argument is that he assumes, without argumentation, that water in Ezekiel's prophecy is metaphorical or a symbol for the Spirit. He doesn't provide any reason *why* he believes this. The "water" could well be a reference to real water, like in the rite of baptism, and the cleansing spoken of brought about by the sprinkling of such water.

Moreover, even if the prophetical image of "water" were intended to be taken metaphorically, at the time of Jesus, it at least came to be interpreted as a reference to real water in an eschatological baptism, as Murray explains above. And it's within this Jewish theological milieu that Jesus gives us the teaching about "water," "the Spirit," and the second birth. Given this Jewish association of Ezekiel's prophetical image of "water" and such an eschatological baptism, it's reasonable to conclude that Jesus was referencing baptism with these images.

Finally, Baker's metaphorical reading of "water" in Jesus' Born Again discourse makes Jesus' teaching unintelligible. Consider that Jesus says we must be born again of water and Spirit to enter God's kingdom. Yet if "water" is a metaphor for the Spirit, as Baker's above argument asserts, then Jesus would be saying, "Unless a person is born again of the Spirit and the Spirit, he can't enter God's kingdom." That makes no sense. Lest we charge Jesus with a lack of intelligibility in his teaching, we must read the "water" as a reference to real water.

"Water" Refers to the Word of God

Interestingly, Baker has a potential escape hatch for the above dilemma. He proposes the idea that the "water" by which someone is said to be reborn refers to God's word. He appeals to 1 Peter 1:23 as evidence.[6] There, St. Peter writes, "You have been born anew, not of perishable seed but of imperishable, *through the living and abiding word of God.*"

Baker also attempts to support this claim with Ephesians 5:25-26, where Paul speaks of Christ cleansing the Church "by the washing of water with the word." He then couples this with John 15:3, where Jesus says, "You are already made clean by the word which I have spoken to you."

When you take into consideration that the second birth elsewhere in Scripture is associated with the word of God, and that the word of God is that which washes us clean, then it seems plausible for a Protestant to conclude that the water in the Born Again discourse refers to the word of God and *not* the waters of baptism.

Immediately, you should be asking yourself, "Well, which is it? Is the 'water' a metaphor for the Spirit, as in the first counterargument, or is it the word of God?"

But putting this aside, the problem with Baker's argument is that it falls prey to the *non sequitur* (Latin, "it does not follow") fallacy, where the conclusion doesn't follow from the premises in an argument.

In this case, Baker's conclusion, "the water in the Born Again discourse *doesn't* refer to baptism," does not follow from his premise, "we are born anew by the word of God." To be born again by the word of God is not exclusive of being born anew through the waters of baptism. It's possible that one can be born again by *both*.

For example, the "word of God" that Peter speaks of in 1 Peter 1:23 is the "good news preached"—the oral preaching that Paul calls the "word of God" in 1 Thessalonians 2:13. It's unreasonable to think Peter would think our second birth is made actual by the apostolic preaching alone and *not* the waters of baptism, since he is the one who commanded those listening on the day of Pentecost to "repent and be baptized" in order that they may receive the forgiveness of sins and the gift of the Holy Spirit (Acts 2:38). This was in response to the people requesting to be saved after hearing the word of God proclaimed to them. So being born anew can come by *both* the word of God and baptism because it's the hearing of the preaching of "the good news" *that leads people to baptism*.

Therefore, Peter is not excluding baptism when he speaks of being born anew through "the living and abiding word of God." In fact, later in the same epistle (3:21), he directly says, "Baptism now saves you." (See chapter three for the discussion of this passage.) For Peter, it's not either "the good news" or baptism; it's *both-and*.

The same reasoning would apply to Paul's statement in Ephesians 5:25-26 and Jesus' statement in John 15:3: We are born anew through *both* the word of God *and* baptism.

Now, Baker might counter here with a different path to justify his thesis that the "water" in John 3:5 is being used figuratively to refer to God's word. He writes,

> Other uses of "water" in the Gospel of John, the New Testament, and even the Old Testament confirm this

> [the metaphorical use of water] to be the case. Water in these instances is often a recurring symbol used for the gospel of salvation or the word of God [he cites John 4:10–14, 7:37–39, 15:3]. . . .
>
> Obviously, John's metaphoric use of "water" gives us sufficient justification for understanding the word "water" in John 3:5 in a figurative manner to mean the word of God and its power to cleanse the sinner through the regenerating work of the Holy Spirit.[7]

Baker goes on to cite other passages in the New Testament where "water" is a metaphor for the word of God: Titus 3:5, John 13:5 with 15:3, and Ephesians 5:26.

What should we make of this argument? Well, not much.

Notice that Baker thinks "water" must be used as a metaphor to mean the word of God in John 3:5 *because* it's used in several places throughout the Bible as a metaphor to mean the word of God. But if we were to follow that logic, we'd have to say the "water" in the stone jars at the wedding at Cana (John 2:7) is simply a metaphor for the word of God, since "water" is used as a metaphor for God's word throughout Scripture. Surely, Baker doesn't want to say that. Thus, Baker can't just assert that the "water" in John 3:5 is metaphorical for the word of God simply because "water" is used metaphorically for the word of God elsewhere. Some other reason, preferably from the text itself, would have to be given.

Water Refers to Our Biological Birth

Another explanation sees the "water" as referring to our biological birth. The second birth, so it's argued, is being born *only* of the Spirit—when you confess Jesus as Lord. Protestant apologist Ron Rhodes explains in his book *Reasoning from the Scriptures with Catholics*:

> Notice how Jesus went about his explanation to Nicodemus. He first speaks about being "born of water and the Spirit" in John 3:5, and then explains what he means by this in verse 6. It would seem that "born of water" in verse 5 is parallel to "born of the flesh" in verse 6, just as "born of the spirit" in verse 5 is parallel to "born of the Spirit" in verse 6. Jesus' message, then, is that just as each person has had a physical birth to live on earth, so he or she must also have a spiritual birth in order to enter the spiritual kingdom of God. A person must be "born from above." Seen in this light, this verse has nothing whatsoever to do with water baptism.[8]

There are some problems with this interpretation. First, the context reveals that Jesus includes *both* Spirit *and* water in the one act of the second birth. He doesn't say, "You must be born of water, and *then* born of the spirit."[9] Protestant scholar Stanley Fowler concurs, writing, "The grammar of the statement seems to link water and spirit closely as two aspects of the same birth (in that the two nouns are objects of one preposition)."[10]

John also has his own way of referring to biological birth, and it doesn't involve water:

> But to all who received him, who believed in his name, he gave power to become children of God; who were born, *not of blood* nor of the will of the flesh nor of the will of man, but of God (John 1:12-13).

John draws a distinction between the new birth of God and biological birth. But he doesn't describe the latter with "water." He speaks of it as "born of blood." So it makes sense that when John records Jesus speaking of birth two different ways in the same conversation—of water, of flesh—he intends to show Jesus making a *contrast* between the two, not using one as a metaphor to clarify the other.

Since we have contextual details that give us good reason to think the birth by water is referring to baptism, and the immediate context of the passage in question already provides language for biological birth that doesn't involve water, it's unreasonable to interpret the birth by water in John 3:3-5 as referring to our biological birth.

Evangelical New Testament scholar D.A. Carson argues as much in his *Gospel According to John*. He writes, "There are no ancient sources that picture natural birth as 'from water.'"[11]

With contextual and scholarly support, therefore, we can conclude that this idea that the "water" refers to our biological birth fails to undermine an appeal to John 3:3-5 as support for baptism being necessary for salvation.

Water Is Material and Doesn't Fit with a Spiritual Birth

Another reason some Christians deny the "water" as being part of the new birth is that it doesn't fit the spiritual nature of the new birth. Here's how the volume on John from *The Preacher's Outline and Sermon Bible* puts it:

> The new birth is spiritual, apart from any natural phenomenon. It has nothing to do with any physical substance, including water. It is not of the flesh, not any material thing. It is of the Spirit.[12]

The "not of the flesh" and "of the Spirit" parts of the above quote are derived from John 3:6, where Jesus says, "That which is born of the flesh is flesh, and that which is born of the Spirit is spirit."

Notice that this interpretation reads into Jesus' words that anything and everything that is material or physical is excluded from being involved in the spiritual rebirth. But that is not what Jesus says.

Rather, Jesus juxtaposes two kinds of *birth*: our physical or natural birth, which is "of the flesh," and the spiritual or supernatural rebirth, which is "of the Spirit." The focus is the essential difference between the births, not what might or might not be involved with those births.

For example, our physical or natural birth is "of the flesh," yet that doesn't mean that anything and everything spiritual is excluded from it, since our natural birth does involve something spiritual—namely, our soul, which animates the matter of our body. But the birth itself is described as "of the flesh" because that's an idiom Jesus frequently uses to express things that pertain to the *natural* order apart from God's grace.

Consider what he says in John 8:15: "You judge according to the flesh." There, Jesus is telling the Pharisees that they judge from an earthly perspective alone.

He also employs this idiom in John 6:63, when he says, "The words that I have spoken to you are spirit and life. The Spirit gives life, the flesh is of no avail." Per John 8:15, Jesus is teaching his disciples that if they judge his teaching to eat his flesh and drink his blood from an earthly perspective alone, they won't be able to assent to it. His teaching goes beyond human reason. Consequently, they need a power that is above reason, which only the Spirit can give, and that's the gift of faith.

So the birth "of the flesh" that Jesus speaks of is our first birth, which is *natural*, and that natural birth doesn't exclude any and all things spiritual, since the soul is present with the body in that first birth.

Our spiritual rebirth, on the other hand, is *not* a physical birth. It is a spiritual birth. That's why Jesus says it is "spirit," or "of the Spirit." But just because the birth is spiritual in nature doesn't necessarily exclude any and everything material.

It may well involve something material, like water, that serves as a means through which the spiritual rebirth takes place.

Consider again John 6:63. Jesus says, "The words that I have spoken to you are spirit and life. The Spirit gives life, the flesh is of no avail." Affirming that his words are spiritual, and are discerned by the Spirit, doesn't mean he didn't use audible sounds, something of the physical world, to communicate his words.

Similarly, just because Jesus teaches that the new birth is spirit and not flesh doesn't mean all fleshy and physical things, like water, are excluded. It simply refers to a particular *kind* of birth that is distinct from our physical birth.

That this is the focus is supported by the fact that Jesus draws this contrast in response to Nicodemus, who thought the new birth was to involve a grown man entering his mother's womb a second time (v. 4).

Therefore, the spiritual nature of the new birth can't be appealed to as evidence for water being excluded from the new birth.

John Uses "Born of God" Without Reference to Water

Another obstacle to seeing ritual water as being part and parcel of the new birth is that John uses the phrase "born of God" elsewhere without reference to water. Again, we turn to Baker for his articulation of this argument. He writes,

> John uses the phrase "born of God" in his first epistle four times (1 John 3:9; 4:7; 5:1, 4) to indicate the new birth produces a sinless nature, a godly love for fellow Christians and one's neighbor, and a supernatural ability to overcome a world hostile to Christ and his faithful followers. 1 John 5:1 declares, "Whoever believes that Jesus is the Christ is born of God," and in that same epistle, where the new birth is frequently mentioned with

> attendant evidences, water baptism is never mentioned as the cause or agent that brings about this spiritual rebirth. It is belief in Jesus the Messiah, and nothing else, which brings about the new birth![13]

Baker's argument seems to be that if John were speaking about baptism as the new birth in 1 John 5:1 (and the other passages), then he would have mentioned water baptism. Since he doesn't, Baker concludes that John *isn't* speaking about baptism as the new birth.

One response is that Baker's inference, yet again, is a *non sequitur.* His conclusion, "John is not talking about water baptism," doesn't necessarily follow from the premise, "John doesn't mention water baptism when speaking about the new birth." It's possible that John assumes that his readers already associate the new birth with water baptism, a tradition that we argue is encoded within his own Gospel—namely, in John 3:3-5. This being the case, there would be no need to mention "water baptism."

A second reason why John wouldn't mention water baptism in these passages is that he wasn't concerned with what *causes* or *brings about* the new birth. In fact, in each of the passages cited, John is concerned about what the child of God manifests *after* he's already born of God. Consider:

- 1 John 3:9: "Anyone born of God *does not* commit sin."
- 1 John 4:7: "Beloved, let us love one another; for love is of God, and he who loves *is* born of God and knows God."
- 1 John 5:1: "Everyone who believes that Jesus is the Christ *has been* born of God."
- 1 John 5:4: "For whatever is born of God *overcomes* the world."

For John, the things listed in these passages—"not committing sin," "loving God and others," "believing in Jesus Christ," and "overcoming the world"—don't make someone born again. Rather, they are the befitting behavior of those who *already* have been spiritually reborn.

Given this context, it's not merely possible, but actually plausible to suggest that where John mentions baptism without mentioning water, he does so assuming that his readers already associate the new birth with water baptism. If the identification of the new birth with water baptism is simply part of the Christian theological air that they breathe, so to speak, then it would be fitting simply to refer to the new birth without reference to water baptism. Then he can talk about the aftereffects of baptism without once more going through the process or the mechanics of it.

For example, when I ask well-formed Catholics, "Are you born again?", they immediately respond, "Yes," because they know that by "born again," I mean "baptized." A similar situation could explain why John doesn't mention water baptism in 1 John 5:1 and the other passages that Baker cites—when his readers heard "new birth," they immediately knew it referred to "water baptism."

The question of what makes someone born again is irrelevant to what John is communicating in the passages where he mentions baptism "of God." Consequently, it's an open question. It *could* be water baptism that he's talking about, or it could not be. These texts can't settle the question one way or the other. It's futile, therefore, for Baker to appeal to these passages as evidence that the new birth is not water baptism.

Baptism Is a Work

So far, the counterarguments have been focused on the "water" mentioned in the Born Again discourse—what the "water" refers to and whether it's part and parcel of the second birth. But there are other tacks a disputant can take.

For example, Baker rejects the baptismal interpretation of the second birth because he views baptism to be a work that merits the initial gift of salvation, which, for him, "contradicts every passage in the Bible where the reader is plainly informed that salvation is a gift of God's unmerited grace, not of works, or anything the sinner does to earn it (e.g., John 3:16; Rom. 10:9–10; Eph. 2:8–9)."[14] If salvation is a gift given by God *not* on account of anything we do, and baptism is a work, then it follows that salvation can't be given through baptism.

Baker makes his argument based on the assumption that Catholics (and all believers in baptismal regeneration) believe that baptism is a work that merits the gift of initial salvation, which, of course, does contradict Ephesians 2:8–9: "For you have been saved by grace and not of works." But this assumption is false. Catholics don't believe that baptism merits the gift of salvation. Rather, we believe that baptism is the *means* stipulated by Christ by which he intends to give us the gift of salvation, not a work that merits the gift. The stipulation of a means doesn't entail an act that merits.

For example, Cy Kellett, the host of *Catholic Answers Live,* often tells those who call in to the show, "We want to give you a book as a gift. Just hang on the line, give us your mailing address, and we'll send it to you." Does the caller's act of giving the call screener his mailing address, receiving the gift in the mail, and opening the package merit the gift? No. The gift is a gift, even if there is a specific way that the recipient must receive it.

Protestants even teach that a person is saved, or justified, on account of a profession of faith—a profession that is often verbalized at an altar call. Yet they don't think such a profession of faith "merits" the gift of salvation, or justification.

Rather, they teach that faith is the *instrument* of justification. Thus, the Catholic view of baptism being the instrument of salvation is no more a meritorious work than a Protestant's view of faith being the instrument of salvation.

Moreover, the interior regeneration that we believe takes place in baptism—the transference from a state of unrighteousness to a state of righteousness—is nothing of our own doing. It is entirely an act of God. *Only* he can bring about such a change within us.

Therefore, according to a Catholic understanding, baptism is a not a work in the way that Baker thinks it is. And given that Baker's argument here is based on a flawed assumption, it has no force against the baptismal interpretation of the second birth.

Spiritual Rebirth Is an Act of God Alone

Baker has another counterargument that latches on to what was said above—namely, that spiritual rebirth is something that *only* God can bring about. He writes,

> Nothing in this world can generate the power of spiritual rebirth; flesh can produce only flesh. Although things in nature, like water, wind, and physical birth, are symbols to picture and describe how spiritual rebirth from God occurs, and the particular effects it has on the person who believes in Jesus Christ for salvation.
>
> Even in the beginning of John's Gospel, the reader is told that the power of spiritual rebirth, whereby the believer in Christ becomes a child of God, is not an act that can be exercised by human act of will, or physical generation, or performance of any kind—the act of sacramental baptism included—but is a supernatural, sovereign act of God alone, bestowed upon those who believe

> in Jesus Christ. Those who are baptized do so by an act of their own will. The new birth is altogether different from this; it is an act of God! . . .
>
> So then, "born of water" in John 3:5 cannot mean the physical rite of baptism as the agent for spiritual rebirth; it must mean something else.[15]

So, for Baker, since the spiritual rebirth is an act of God, it cannot involve any human act. And since the ritual of water baptism involves a human act, it follows that the spiritual rebirth can't be a reference to ritual water baptism.

The problem with this line of reasoning is that it would preclude humans being involved in several things that the Bible affirms humans *are* involved in when God exercises his sovereignty.

Consider, for example, the healing of the lame beggar that Peter performs in Acts 3:1-10. The effect of the miracle can be brought about only by God. Yet that doesn't mean Peter's action isn't involved. God used Peter as an instrumental cause to bring about the miraculous effect.

Consider also Paul's teaching that we are justified by "faith." Faith is a gift that God alone can give. Yet the act of faith itself, which God moves us to engage in, involves the act of our intellect, moved by the will, to assent to what God reveals and the act of directing our hearts and minds to God as our ultimate supernatural end. That's human action, actualized within us by God.

More examples abound. In John 16:8, we're told that the Spirit will convict the world of sin and righteousness. However, we know that the Spirit uses preachers to establish that conviction. Life itself is from God, yet God uses the actions of a human mother and father to be participants in giving that life to us.

One more example, which perhaps relates best to our topic at hand: Jesus heals the blind man in John 9:1-7. And he intentionally involves the blind man's action—namely, Jesus commands him to go and wash his eyes in the pool of Siloam. Once the blind man does that human act, Jesus heals him.

So just because an effect is brought about by God alone, like the spiritual rebirth, that doesn't necessarily exclude human action, like ritual water baptism. It's God's prerogative to will ritual water baptism to be the *means* or *instrument* through which *he* communicates the blessing. Given the positive evidence presented above that Jesus intends the second birth to refer to baptism, we know that God *in fact* wills ritual water baptism to be such a means.

Nicodemus Wouldn't Have Known About Sacramental Baptism

The above commentary *John: The Preacher's Outline and Sermon Bible* presents another interesting counterargument. The authors argue that the baptismal interpretation of the second birth wouldn't make sense given Nicodemus's lack of knowledge about sacramental baptism:

> Is it possible that water means "baptism" here? When John was writing the Gospel, he and the readers of his Gospel would have known what was meant by Christian baptism. However, when Jesus was speaking to Nicodemus, there was no such thing as Christian baptism.
>
> It is unlikely that Jesus would say something that Nicodemus could not grasp and understand. Jesus was not one to confuse him, but to lead him to be born again. There was no way Nicodemus could be baptized in order to be born again—not then—for Christian baptism had not yet been instituted.[16]

That Christian baptism had not yet been instituted is irrelevant. Of course it hadn't. Jesus was revealing it here for the first time, we argue. The mere lack of prior awareness of something doesn't preclude someone grasping and understanding the new revelation given.

The real issue is whether Nicodemus would have been properly disposed to grasp and understand the reference to sacramental baptism. Well, given what we argued above concerning the Jewish interpretation of Ezekiel 36:25-27 as a reference to an eschatological ritual water baptism, we can conclude that Nicodemus *would* have been properly disposed to grasp and understand the "water and Spirit" as a reference to ritual water baptism. He would even be able to grasp the *spiritual* nature of the new birth—that's to say, it's something distinct from a physical birth.

Of course, the precise *nature* of regeneration in the new birth (e.g., transference from a state of unrighteousness to a state of righteousness with the theological virtues of faith, hope, and charity that come with sanctifying/habitual grace) would require further elaboration. But that's not necessary for Nicodemus to grasp the idea that Jesus' ritual water baptism brings about a spiritual renewal and that such a renewal is necessary for entrance into the kingdom of God, which is the minimum we need for evidence that Jesus is revealing sacramental baptism.

This is not at all different from Jesus telling Nicodemus about the "kingdom of God" without specifying the precise nature of what membership in the kingdom means—having sanctifying grace in the soul at a minimum, and the maximum being the beatific vision in heaven. Surely, Nicodemus wasn't yet disposed to grasp and understand these aspects of membership in the kingdom. Yet Jesus still spoke of it in the general terms of the "kingdom of God." Similarly, Jesus can speak of sacramental baptism in the general terms of new birth by "water and Spirit" without specifying the precise nature of that new birth.

One final thought. Why must we assume that Nicodemus would have to understand Jesus' revelation right away? Several times in his ministry, Jesus revealed things that his apostles didn't immediately understand and came to understand only later. Jesus' resurrection is one such example. In Mark 9:31, Jesus tells the disciples, "The Son of man will be delivered into the hands of men, and they will kill him; and when he is killed, after three days he will rise." Mark then comments, "But they did not understand the saying, and they were afraid to ask him" (v. 32).

John later confirms this lack of understanding and tells us that only later did he come to understand. In his recounting of Peter and himself going to see Jesus' empty tomb, he writes, "Then the other disciple [John], who reached the tomb first, also went in, and he saw and believed; for as yet they did not know the Scripture, that he must rise from the dead" (John 20:8-9).

Given these data, we can simply reject the underlying principle that drives the above argument—namely, that Jesus wouldn't say something to Nicodemus that he couldn't grasp and understand. There are times when Jesus reveals something that's vague and cryptic for his disciples, only later to illuminate their minds.

Jesus Didn't Baptize Anyone

The remaining two counterarguments to the sacramental interpretation of the new birth are two sides of the same coin, both of which come from Baker. They're both based on the expectation of what Jesus would and wouldn't do if he intended the new birth to be a reference to sacramental baptism. Let's start with the expectation of what Jesus would have done if he had intended the new birth to be a reference to baptism.

Baker argues as follows: "If Jesus meant to teach water baptism was necessary for salvation in John 3:5, he *would* have baptized every single person who came to him in faith."[17] His reason for thinking this? "This would be quite disturbing and troubling, if John 3:5 had Jesus teaching water baptism was necessary for salvation, and then the very Author of that salvation, did not himself baptize anybody!" Since Jesus didn't baptize anyone, Baker argues, it follows that Jesus didn't teach in John 3:5 that water baptism is necessary for salvation.

One problem with Baker's line of reasoning is that he thinks that for baptism to be necessary for salvation, Jesus must be the one administering it. And the only reason that Baker gives for this is that it's "quite disturbing and troubling" to imagine Jesus personally "withholding" baptism from those whose eternal life depended on receiving it.

Well, it's not disturbing and troubling for Catholics and others who believe in baptismal regeneration. Logically speaking, baptism *could* be necessary for salvation, and Jesus could *also* will for only *his disciples* to be the ones to administer it.

As an analogy, belief that the books in our bibles, both Jewish (Old Testament) and Christian (New Testament), are inspired is necessary for salvation (at least for those to whom it is revealed). Yet Jesus never wrote anything. He willed that his disciples do that.

Also, *all* revealed truth from God the Father is necessary for salvation (again, at least for those to whom it is revealed). Yet Jesus explicitly tells his apostles that *he will not* be the one to give them the completeness of that revelation. Rather, the Holy Spirit will serve that role. John records Jesus saying, "These things I have spoken to you, while I am still with you.

But the Counselor, the Holy Spirit, whom the Father will send in my name, he will teach you all things, and bring to your remembrance all that I have said to you" (John 14:26).

Notice the juxtaposition between "these things" and "*all* things." The implication is that there are some things the Holy Spirit will teach the disciples that Jesus did not while he was with them. Must we conclude that what the Holy Spirit brings to their minds isn't necessary for salvation, since Jesus wasn't the one teaching it? Baker's logic would have us say yes. But that's absurd!

Now, someone might ask, "What's an example of a truth that Jesus didn't teach the apostles but that the Holy Spirit did?" Circumcision doesn't save! Such a truth came about by the Holy Spirit providentially guiding the early Church to declare it through the means of a council in Acts 15.

Given that we have biblical precedent for Jesus willing not to administer a gift with that gift nonetheless being necessary for salvation, we can conclude that baptism could be necessary for salvation without Jesus administering it himself. Baker's argument, therefore, is unsuccessful.

Jesus Saved People Without Baptism

I mentioned above that there's another counterargument that is the flip side of the above one. Baker asks, "If Jesus demanded water baptism for salvation, as proposed by Rome, why then did he forgive and save people in his ministry without the requirement of baptismal regeneration?"[18] For an example, he appeals to Jesus in Luke 7:47-50 forgiving the sins of the woman of disrepute. Jesus declares her sins "forgiven" (v. 48) and says her "faith has saved" her (v. 49). For Baker, this proves that baptism isn't necessary for salvation. And if that's the case, then Jesus can't possibly be speaking of baptism in John 3:5.

There are two possible ways to interpret Baker's argument here. If he's saying this event shows that baptism isn't necessary for salvation in a strict, absolute sense, then we agree. As will be explained later in more detail (chapter ten), the Church affirms that God can save people without the sacrament of baptism. The *Catechism of the Catholic Church* teaches as much:

> The Lord himself affirms that baptism is necessary for salvation. He also commands his disciples to proclaim the gospel to all nations and to baptize them. Baptism is necessary for salvation for those to whom the gospel has been proclaimed and who have had the possibility of asking for this sacrament.
>
> The Church does not know of any means other than baptism that assures entry into eternal beatitude; this is why she takes care not to neglect the mission she has received from the Lord to see that all who can be baptized are "reborn of water and the Spirit." *God has bound salvation to the sacrament of Baptism, but he himself is not bound by his sacraments* (1257).[19]

If, however, Baker's argument is intended to be taken in a less strict way, simply to say that it's strange on the view that baptism is necessary for salvation that Jesus' common pattern of saving people is without baptism, then we have a few answers.

First, it's reasonable that Jesus wouldn't save this woman through the means of baptism because sacramental baptism had not yet been established as the ordinary means of salvation. Remember, Jesus didn't necessarily will the beginning of the actual practice of sacramental baptism in John 3:5; he merely instituted it in the sense of revealing its role in the New Covenant economy of salvation. Perhaps Jesus didn't intend the sacramental economy to be actualized until after Pentecost, which is the common teaching of theologians throughout history.

A second possible response is that even if the practice of sacramental baptism were already in place as the ordinary means of salvation, Jesus can still save people without the sacrament in extraordinary circumstances to achieve some purpose or end. In this case, it's possible that Jesus wanted to publicly make his claim to have power to forgive sins and thereby align himself with God the Father concerning divine power. This end wouldn't have been achieved if he were to have waited to save her through the means of sacramental baptism. Moreover, Jesus could have been intending to teach us that although he binds us to the sacrament of baptism as the ordinary means of salvation, he himself (as God) is not bound to the sacrament to save, which is exactly what the above quote from the *Catechism* teaches.

So on either account of Baker's argument, the argument doesn't succeed to show that the new birth in John 3:5 isn't a reference to sacramental baptism.

Conclusion

As this chapter has shown, there is no shortage of counterarguments to the exegesis that the new birth by "water and Spirit" is a reference to sacramental baptism. Whether it's an alternative reading of the term "water," or what the Bible says elsewhere about the new birth, or what Jesus did and didn't do, we've shown why they all fail to disprove the baptismal reading of the new birth by "water and Spirit" in John 3:5. And when we add to this that we have positive lines of reasoning to support the baptismal interpretation, we can conclude that *Jesus* teaches that the sacrament of baptism regenerates us—that's to say, it saves us.

But are we Catholics, and other believers in baptismal regeneration, all alone when it comes to the belief that baptism saves? What do Ss. Peter and Paul have to say about it? What does the early Church have to say about it?

The answers to these questions will be the focus of the next few chapters. Let's begin with Paul.

CHAPTER 2

St. Paul Says So

There aren't too many passages where Paul speaks about baptism. However, in the passages where he does mention it, his theology is profound and worth unpacking. The two passages that we will look at are 1 Corinthians 12:13 and Romans 6:3-4, 7, 17-18, the passage from Romans 6 being the clearest and strongest text.

1 Corinthians 12:13

Let's start with 1 Corinthians 12:13, where Paul writes, "For by one Spirit we were all baptized into one body." The "body" that Paul speaks of here is "the body of Christ." The context involves Paul comparing the union of Christians in Christ to members of a physical body. He begins in verse 12: "As a body is one though it has many parts, and all the parts of the body, though many, are one body, so also Christ." Then, in verse 27, he identifies the body that all Christians make up with this body of Christ, saying, "Now you are Christ's body, and individually parts of it." Given that the "body" Paul speaks of in verse 13 refers to "Christ's body," and baptism incorporates us into that body, it follows that baptism incorporates us into the "body of Christ."

The question, however, is whether by "body of Christ" Paul means simply the visible corporate body of believers, a common interpretation among some Protestants, or the *mystical* body of Christ, which is constituted by believers united via grace. The latter view is the Catholic view, which the Orthodox and others also hold. If Paul intends *this* view, then we have revelation of the salvific efficacy of baptism, since to be "in Christ" is not to be subject to condemnation, as Paul teaches in Romans 8:1 ("There is therefore now no condemnation for those who are in Christ Jesus"). We argue that Paul intends this latter view: baptism incorporates us into the *mystical* body of Christ.

I think the key is the analogy of the body. Paul compares each member of Christ's body, which refers to Christians, with each member of a physical body. Now, each member of a physical body doesn't live with its own life. Rather, it lives with the life of the person whose body the member is a part of, such that if a member gets cut off from the body, it's dead and no longer living with the life of the person. It's this single life of the person, which flows through each member of his body, that unites all the members, such that one member can assist the others.

Given that Paul compares the union that Christians have with this sort of union, we can conclude that Paul envisions Christians living spiritually not with a life of their own, but with the life of the person whose body they are a part of—namely, Christ. There is a mystical union among Christians *in Christ* that Paul envisions here, a union established by God's grace dwelling within each Christian.

Since baptism incorporates us into that mystical union in Christ, and that union in Christ is a state of salvation (being free from condemnation), it follows that baptism saves.

Romans 6:3-4, 7, 17-18

The next passage where we find Paul's teaching on baptism is Romans 6:3-4, 7, and 17-18. Paul starts in verses 3-4, writing,

> Do you not know that all of us who have been baptized into Christ Jesus were baptized into his death? We were buried therefore with him by baptism into death, so that as Christ was raised from the dead by the glory of the Father, we too might walk in newness of life.

He goes on to articulate the effects of this baptismal death and resurrection:

> We know that our old self was crucified with him so that the sinful body might be destroyed, and we might no longer be enslaved to sin. For he who has died is freed from sin (vv. 6-7).

What's interesting about this passage, as pointed out in Catholic circles by apologist Jimmy Akin, is that the original biblical text in Greek doesn't say "freed from sin." The Greek verb translated "freed" is *dikaioō*, which means "to put into a right relationship (with God); acquit, declare and treat as righteous."[20] This is the same verb Paul uses when he speaks of our justification by faith: "Since we are justified [Greek, *dikaiōthentes*] by faith, we have peace with God through our Lord Jesus Christ" (Rom. 5:1). So the phrase "freed from sin" in Romans 6:7 can literally be translated "justified from sin." And such justification is the peace that we have with God as Christians—to be in a right relationship with him, or to be saved.

Modern translations render verse 7 as "freed from sin" because the context is clearly about sanctification. For example, in the verse before Paul speaks of baptismal death, he speaks of those in Christ as having "died to sin." As quoted above, Paul speaks of those who have died the death of baptism as "no longer enslaved to sin."

In verses 17-18, Paul actually uses a form of the Greek word for "free" (*eleutheroō*) in relation to the freedom from sin that we receive in Christ:

> But thanks be to God, that you who were once slaves of sin have become obedient from the heart to the standard of teaching to which you were committed, and, having been set free [Greek, *eleutherōthentes*] from sin, have become slaves of righteousness.

Paul's teaching about the freedom from sin through the baptismal death tells us that, for Paul, justification includes sanctification, which is the interior renewal of the soul whereby the objective guilt of sin is removed. And that justification, or salvation, takes place *in baptism.*

Now, the above verses (vv. 17-18) specifically also support the thesis that Paul sees the baptismal death as justifying us. Consider that the Greek word for "righteousness" is *dikaiosunē*, which is related to the verb (*dikaioō*) that Paul used above in verse 7. It's also the word that Paul uses in Romans 4:2-5 when he describes Abraham's justification by faith:

> For if Abraham was justified by works, he has something to boast about, but not before God. For what does the Scripture say? "Abraham believed God, and it was reckoned to him as righteousness" [Greek, *dikaiosunēn*]. Now to one who works, his wages are not reckoned as a gift but as his due. And to one who does not work but trusts him who justifies the ungodly, his faith is reckoned as righteousness [Greek, *dikaiosunēn*].

So for Paul, the state of being "slaves of righteousness" is a state of being justified, like Abraham. Since for Paul it's the baptismal death and resurrection that bring about such a state of justification, it follows that Paul believed that baptism justifies us—that's to say, it saves us. And if Paul believed it, then so should we.

As to the *nature* of this justification or salvation, we saw above in verse 7 that Paul identifies justification with sanctification, thereby excluding the idea that justification is merely a legal declaration by God. Verses 17–18 serve this same end.

Notice that in verses 17–18, Paul describes two states, both of which are preceded by and contrasted with the same state of slavery to sin. First, he speaks of becoming "obedient from the heart," as opposed to being "slaves of sin." Second, he speaks of "slaves of righteousness" who were "set free from sin"—which is to say his addressees went from being slaves of sin to being slaves of righteousness.

Given this "common denominator" of slavery to sin, it's clear that Paul is describing in two different ways the same state that is opposite being a slave to sin. This being the case, Paul doesn't see a hard divide between the state of "obedience from the heart" and the state of being "slaves of righteousness." In fact, he conceives of them as one and the same.

Here's where the understanding of interior righteousness (brought about through regeneration) comes into play. Consider that obedience to God ("obedience from the heart") entails the mind and the will being rightly ordered to God's will—being disposed to believe as true what he says and to do what he commands. That's an interior state—a state that's constitutive of our character.

It's this interior state of the heart and mind, a state that God brings about within us by grace, that Paul identifies as the state of being "slaves of righteousness," which, as we saw above, is a state of justification, like that of Abraham. Therefore, interior righteousness, or what the Council of Trent called the "justice within us," is grounds for our justification at least to some extent.[21]

So not only do we have evidence that Paul believed that baptism justifies us. He also believed that such justification is a spiritual renewal within us, freeing us from the slavery of sin. Put those two things together, and we have regeneration by water and Spirit, according to Paul.

Now, as it was with John 3:5, Christians who reject baptismal regeneration can't concede the above exegesis. So the question becomes, "How might a Protestant counter?" Our friend Todd Baker has a few ideas. He challenges the above assumption that by "baptism" Paul means ritual water baptism. Baker argues that Paul doesn't intend water baptism, and he gives two reasons for his conclusion. We will deal with each in turn.

Paul Doesn't Say Anything About Water

The first reason Baker gives for why Paul isn't talking about water baptism here is that Paul doesn't say anything about water. He states the argument this way:

> Paul's use of baptism in Romans 6:3-5 does not mention water anywhere, and therefore can conceivably convey the greater idea of identification with Christ in his death and resurrection for the sinner's salvation, without necessarily pointing to the idea of the rite or act of water baptism. . . .
>
> If Paul means a water and ritual baptism in Romans 6, he would have clearly included the term "water" as the descriptive modifier to baptism, which he does not. Consequently, the Apostle would have written Romans 6:3-4, if water baptism were the productive means of salvation and union with Jesus Christ, to read: "As many of

> us were immersed (baptized) into water in Christ were immersed into water into his death. Therefore we are buried with him by immersing in water into his death."[22]

For Baker, what Paul intends by the term "baptism" is not water baptism, but what constitutes our salvation—namely, union with Christ. Is Baker right that Paul is *not* referring to water baptism here?

Notice the reason why Baker thinks Paul is not referring to water baptism: He doesn't include the term "water." But this is an unreasonable expectation.

Paul wrote his letter to the Romans around A.D. 54. That means that for roughly twenty years, Christians would have been practicing water baptism in obedience to Christ's command in Matthew 28:19 to baptize. And we have evidence that they practiced water baptism from the get-go (see Acts 8:16; 10:48; 11:14; 16:15, 33; 18:8 and 1 Cor. 1:16).

This means that for Christians, the term "baptism" would have already denoted *water* baptism, and thus there would have been no need for Paul to modify "baptism" with the term "water." Just as *we* don't have to use the term "water" when referring to the ritual washing of baptism, so too Paul didn't need to use the term "water" when referring to the rite of water baptism. "Baptism" sufficed. Besides, what else would Christians think of by the term "baptism"?

Now, if Baker were to counter and say that Paul must be referring to something else besides "water" baptism because baptism is merely a symbol of our union with Christ, then he'd be begging the question against the Christian who appeals to Romans 6:3-7, 17-18 as evidence for Paul's belief in the salvific nature of baptism. You can't reject a passage that we say reveals that baptism is more than a symbol because you believe that baptism is nothing more than a symbol.

Furthermore, Protestant scholar Douglas Moo argues that "baptism" at this time was equated with water baptism. He writes,

> By the date of Romans, "baptize" had become almost a technical expression for the rite of Christian initiation by water, and this is surely the meaning of the Roman Christians would have given the word.[23]

So, given Baker's unreasonable expectation that Paul use "water" in this text when he speaks of baptism, we can reject this counterargument.

Paul Says We're Baptized into Christ

Now, Baker might counter and say that we don't need to rely on what we might expect Paul to say or not say. We can appeal to what he *does* say. For Baker, Paul isn't referring to ritual water baptism because the baptism spoken of is "into Christ," not water. Here's his argument in full:

> The key to understanding the nature of what Paul means here by reference to baptism is tied up with the Greek preposition *eis* (εἰς), which means "into," and its integral relation to "baptism." It is simply what the text of Romans 6:3-4 says it is: a baptism into Christ (into his death and resurrection), not a baptism into water; water baptism does symbolize such a union or identification, but does not produce this saving union with Christ.
>
> To merely assume that Romans 6:3-4 is speaking about the ritual of water baptism is to force that idea into the text when it clearly speaks of a baptism into Christ, not a baptism of water. . . .
>
> The meaning of spiritual baptism in Christ, rather than water baptism, fits the context of Romans 6 better, when

> one realizes that "a baptism into water (not taking out) is impossible; a baptism into Christ (not taking out) is the very demand of salvation."[24]

I see two problems with Baker's argument. First, it's a bit odd to expect Paul to say we're baptized *into* water if he were envisioning the ritual act of washing *with* water, since that would entail Paul saying water baptism baptizes us into water, which is absurd.

Second, Baker concludes that Paul isn't speaking of water baptism because Paul doesn't say we're baptized into water. But the question at hand doesn't concern that into which we're baptized. Rather, the issue is the nature of the "baptism" that brings about whatever we're baptized into. In other words, the question is whether the activity signified by the term "baptism" is the ritual act of washing with water or something else. *That's* what we're debating. So what we're baptized into, whether Christ or water, is irrelevant as to the nature of the "baptism" that Paul envisions.

This leads to a third problem. Baker assumes that being baptized "into Christ" is restricted to a purely spiritual reading of the term "baptism." But the effect of being incorporated "into Christ" can just as easily fit with a sacramental reading. In fact, Christians who believe in the salvific efficacy of baptism believe that baptism brings about incorporation into the mystical body of Christ. Consider, for example, the *Catechism*. In paragraph 1267, it states, "Baptism makes us members of the Body of Christ" and then quotes Ephesians 4:25 for support: "Therefore . . . we are members one of another."

Baker argues in the above quote that to interpret Paul's words as a reference to water baptism is to "force that idea into the text." But in fact, it's Baker who forces his spiritual baptism view into the text, at least on the grounds that we're baptized into Christ.

Paul Didn't Come to Baptize (1 Cor. 1:17)

The next counter isn't directed specifically at our exegesis of Romans 6:3–4. Rather, it's more of a general argument against the view that Paul believed that baptism saves. It comes from 1 Corinthians 1:17. Paul writes, "For Christ did not send me to baptize but to preach the gospel, and not with eloquent wisdom, lest the cross of Christ be emptied of its power."

Those who appeal to this verse argue that Paul dissociates baptism from the gospel. And if baptism is not part of the gospel, it can't be necessary for salvation.[25] There are three ways to respond.

First, the challenge confuses the duty to *administer* the rite of baptism with baptism being essential to the gospel. Paul doesn't say that baptism is not essential to the gospel. What does and doesn't constitute the gospel isn't Paul's concern here. Rather, he is concerned with the *administration* of baptism.

Paul is addressing a problem that arose in the Corinthian church, where some were identifying themselves with particular ministers and causing division within the community. Paul writes,

> It has been reported to me by Chloe's people that there is quarreling among you, my brethren. What I mean is that each one of you says, "I belong to Paul," or "I belong to Apollos," or "I belong to Cephas," or "I belong to Christ" (1 Cor. 1:11).

In subsequent verses, Paul gives a hint as to why the Corinthians were identifying themselves with different ministers:

> Were you baptized in the name of Paul? I am thankful that I baptized none of you except Crispus and Gaius; lest anyone should say that you were baptized in my name (vv.13-14).

Apparently, the Corinthians were adopting religious affiliations based on the minister who *baptized* them. Consequently, Paul was grateful that he hadn't baptized more people than he had among the Corinthians, lest they affiliate themselves with him.

It is within this context that Paul says, "For Christ did not send me to baptize but to preach the gospel" (1 Cor. 1:17). His intent is not to separate the sacrament of baptism from the gospel, but rather to clarify his own part in the *administration* of the actual rite of baptism among the Corinthians.

Even if we conceded, for argument's sake, that Paul was sent in a strict sense not to baptize, it doesn't follow that baptism is not essential to the gospel. Paul's preaching of the gospel could have included the necessity of baptism for salvation—with the administration of the actual rite of baptism left to other ministers. Someone other than Paul performing baptism wouldn't prevent baptism from being essential to the gospel message that Paul preached.

But as we'll see, we have good reason to not take Paul's statement in a strict sense. This leads to our second response. Paul is using hyperbole to emphasize two things:

1. It doesn't matter by whom you're baptized, and
2. His apostolic role is not restricted to administering baptism but also involves preaching the gospel.

We know that Paul's statement, "For Christ did not send me to baptize," is hyperbolic because Jesus commanded *all* the apostles to make disciples of all nations by baptizing them

(Matt. 28:19–20). And since Paul is an apostle, it therefore belongs to his ministry to baptize.

Moreover, if Paul wasn't sent to baptize in a strict sense, then he would have acted in disobedience when he baptized Crispus, Gaius, and the household of Stephanas, which he tells us about in verse 14. Do we want to say that the great apostle Paul was disobedient to Jesus' instruction?

With this hyperbolic speech, Paul is stressing that it doesn't matter by whom you're baptized. Whether it's Apollos, Cephas, or Paul who baptizes, we're all incorporated into the same "fellowship of [God's] Son, Jesus Christ our Lord" (1 Cor. 1:9).

The use of hyperbole is similar to Jesus' teaching in John 12:44: "He who believes in me, believes not in me but in him who sent me." Of course, Jesus doesn't mean that we shouldn't believe in *him*. With the "not . . . but" formula, he is merely emphasizing the importance of the Father's authority with which he is sent, and consequently that we shouldn't believe in Jesus *alone*, but also in the Father.[26]

This is the same kind of language that Paul uses in 1 Corinthians 1:17: "For Christ *did not* send me to baptize *but* to preach the gospel." Paul uses this "not . . . but" formula elsewhere when employing hyperbole. Consider, for example, 1 Corinthians 15:10. He writes, "But by the grace of God I am what I am, and his grace toward me was not in vain. On the contrary, I worked harder than any of them, though it was *not I, but the grace of God* which is with me." Surely, Paul didn't intend to say that his work literally was not the product of his own will. Rather, he was emphasizing the *primacy* of God's grace.

Paul's first letter to the Thessalonians is another example. He writes in verse 7 of chapter 4, "For God has not called us for uncleanness, but in holiness." Then he says, "Therefore whoever disregards this, disregards *not man but God*, who gives his Holy Spirit to you." Is Paul saying that someone who disregards this teaching is literally *not* disregarding Paul, who is giving the teaching? Of course not! Paul's using hyperbolic speech to emphasize the point that to reject this teaching is ultimately to reject God because the teaching comes from God.

We have good reason, therefore, to interpret Paul's "not . . . but" formula as hyperbole.

A third response is that the assertion that baptism is not essential to the gospel is inconsistent with Paul's above teaching on baptism in Romans 6:3-18. Recall, Paul teaches that through baptism we are "justified from sin"—set free from the slavery to sin—and become "slaves of righteousness." In other words, baptism is the means by which we are justified and sanctified (made holy). Since justification and sanctification are essential to the gospel, and for Paul baptism justifies and sanctifies, it follows that for Paul, baptism *is* essential to the gospel.

We might add: Paul's teaching in Romans 6:3-4 about baptism freeing us from sin may follow from his experience of being forgiven of his sins through baptism in Acts 22:16: "And now why do you wait? Rise and be baptized, and *wash away your sins*, calling on his name."

Conclusion

We started this book with our own baptismal reading of Jesus' teaching about regeneration (the new birth) by water and Spirit. But after consulting 1 Corinthians 12:13 and Romans 6:3-7, 17-18, we can conclude that such a reading has Paul as an ally. Like Jesus, Paul teaches that ritual water baptism transfers us from the old state of slavery to sin to a new state of righteousness, or justification. Such a renewal is essentially what we call *regeneration*, or what Jesus calls "new birth." However, Paul here teases out the implication of the new birth—namely, the passage from spiritual death and slavery to spiritual life and freedom.

With Paul's theology in place, we now ask, "What does St. Peter have to say about baptism?" To that we turn in our next chapter.

Chapter 3

St. Peter Says So

So far, we've appealed to Jesus and St. Paul for evidence that baptism saves. But St. Peter has something to say about it as well. There are two passages where Peter speaks of baptism: Acts 2:38 and 1 Peter 3:21. We will deal with each in turn.

Acts 2:38

Acts 2:38 comes within the context of the Jewish feast of Pentecost, where Peter preached the first sermon for the new-born Christian Church, proclaiming Jesus to be the risen Jewish Messiah (vv. 14-36). Luke tells us that when the crowd "heard this they were cut to the heart, and said to Peter and the rest of the apostles, 'Brethren, what shall we do?'" Peter answered as follows: "Repent, and be baptized every one of you in the name of Jesus Christ *for the forgiveness of your sins*; and you shall receive the gift of the Holy Spirit" (v. 38).

Peter's teaching here is like that of Paul in Romans 6—through water baptism we are forgiven of our sins, which entails inner renewal. However, Peter adds an extra tidbit, saying that we *also* receive the Holy Spirit.

Now, to be forgiven of sins and to receive God's Spirit are tantamount to being saved. For Peter, therefore, baptism is not *just* a symbol of our salvation. Rather, he believes that baptism *brings about* our salvation.

Moreover, notice that we have here water, inner renewal, and God's Spirit. Sounds a lot like Jesus' Born-Again discourse (John 3:5). For Peter, baptism *is* the new birth.

There aren't many comebacks made to this argument by those Protestants who deny the spiritual efficacy of baptism. However, there are a couple, and they need to be answered.

Baptism Isn't the Cause of Salvation, but Rather Follows It

Ron Rhodes bases this argument[27] on a particular reading of the Greek preposition *eis*, translated as "for." Rhodes rightly points out that *eis* "can indicate causality ('in order to attain') or a result ('because of')." An example of the causal sense is, "I'm going to the office for (in order to get) my paycheck." An example of the resultant sense is, "I'm taking an aspirin for (because of) my headache."

Rhodes asserts that in Acts 2:38, *eis* is used in the resultant sense: Peter is *not* saying, "Repent, and be baptized *in order to attain* the forgiveness of sins" but rather, "Repent, and be baptized *because* you've been forgiven." Rather than baptism being a cause of salvation, it's something we do once we're saved.

An immediate problem with this interpretation is that there's no argument here from the verse itself or the immediate context as to why *eis* should be interpreted in the resultant sense in this passage. The only way to support such an interpretation is to go outside the text and appeal to a preconceived thesis that the New Testament pattern for salvation is salvation first, then baptism, which Rhodes does. This alleged pattern will be taken up in our next comeback below.

A second problem is that this interpretation conflicts with the consistent teaching from early Christianity concerning the relationship between baptism and the forgiveness of sins. As will be shown in our next chapter, the early Christians, from the first century on, viewed baptism as *bringing about* the forgiveness of sins. Given the early Church Fathers' witness to such a sacred Christian tradition, we would be within our rights to interpret Acts 2:38 accordingly and reject Rhodes's interpretation.

Here's a third problem: The data in the verse itself, along with its immediate context, give credence to a causal interpretation of "for." In the subsequent verses, you'll notice that nowhere does it say those listening to Peter were forgiven their sins before they received baptism. That's only an assumption.

Verse 37 merely tells us the crowd mourn Peter's indictment of their sin of crucifying their Messiah ("they were cut to the heart") and ask what must be done. Peter responds by instructing the people to repent and be baptized for the forgiveness of their sins, speaks of the promise to them and their children, and further exhorts them to save themselves from their crooked generation. Verse 41 then tells us 3,000 people received Peter's word and were baptized. Nowhere does it say they were forgiven for their sins before they were baptized.

This leads to a fourth problem: The "resultant" interpretation entails unnecessary mental gymnastics when reading the flow of Peter's instructions.[28] We would need to envision repentance, then move forward in time to baptism, then conceptually move back in time to repentance again when we come to the forgiveness of sins, and then move forward again to the future with regard to the reception of the Holy Spirit. That's a strained reading, to say the least. The more natural reading of the text is simply to take all the parts as referring to the future: repentance, and then baptism, and then with baptism the forgiveness of sins and the reception of the Holy Spirit.

Now, a potential counter to the above two critiques might be that the forgiveness of sins is *implied* in the act of repentance. So when the 3,000 repented in response to Peter's instruction, their sins were forgiven, and *then* they were baptized. But that would conflict with the natural flow of Peter's instruction, which makes *both* repentance *and* baptism conditions for receiving the forgiveness of sins. Such an interpretation would be an unnecessarily strained reading of the text, making baptism *not* a condition for the forgiveness of sins when the structure of the sentence itself suggests that it is.

Since there's no evidence that the sins of the 3,000 were forgiven before they received baptism, and we know that Peter links baptism with the forgiveness of sins (1 Pet. 3:21), the natural reading of the text is that the forgiveness of sins *occurs with* the reception of baptism.

Finally, this counterargument fails to consider that Peter links the reception of the Holy Spirit with baptism as an effect to a cause. He says, "Repent, and be baptized . . . and *you shall receive* [Greek, *lēmpsesthe*—future tense] the gift of the Holy Spirit" (Acts 2:38). For Peter, the reception of the Holy Spirit is an *effect* of baptism. And if the Holy Spirit is an effect of baptism, then so too the forgiveness of sins, since the forgiveness of sins comes with the Holy Spirit, at least within the context of obtaining salvation, which, as Rhodes acknowledges, is what Acts 2:38 is all about.

The New Testament's Pattern for Salvation Is Repentance, Faith, and Then Baptism. It's Salvation First, Then Baptism.

I mentioned above that the only way to support the resultant sense of Acts 2:38 is to appeal to the preconceived thesis that the New Testament pattern for salvation is "salvation first, then baptism." There is nothing wrong with allowing prior established revealed principles to govern your interpretation of a certain text. However, your interpretation of that text is only as good as the alleged prior established revealed principles.

In the case we're considering here, the alleged prior revealed principle is that the New Testament pattern for salvation is "salvation first, then baptism." There are several passages that Christians appeal to for evidence.

Rhodes appeals to Acts 10:47–48, where Peter instructs Cornelius and a group of Gentiles to be baptized *after* they receive the Holy Spirit, the assumption being that to receive the Holy Spirit is to be saved (cf. Rom. 8:9): "'Can anyone forbid water for baptizing these people who have received the Holy Spirit just as we have?' And he commanded them to be baptized in the name of Jesus Christ."[29]

In response, this challenge assumes that because Cornelius and his companions received the Holy Spirit, they were saved. But receiving an outpouring of the Holy Spirit doesn't necessarily mean someone is saved.

Consider, first of all, that the Spirit can be given for other things besides salvation.[30] One such thing is artistic skill. For example, God fills Bezalel, son of Uri, with "the Spirit of God" (Exod. 31:3) "to devise artistic designs, to work in gold, silver, and bronze, in cutting stones for setting, and in carving wood, for work in every craft" (vv. 4-5).

To others, God gave his Spirit to empower them with special strength, as exemplified in the life of Samson (Judges 14:6, 19; 15:14) and to empower for leadership (see Num. 27:18; Deut. 34:9; Judges 3:10; 6:34; 11:29; 1 Sam. 11:6-7; 16:13-14).

That the outpouring of the Spirit doesn't guarantee salvation is also evidenced in the New Testament. Consider, for example, Matthew 7:22-23:[31]

> On that day many will say to me, "Lord, Lord, did we not prophesy in your name, and cast out demons in your

> name, and do many mighty works in your name?" And then will I declare to them, "I never knew you; depart from me, you evildoers."

To prophesy and cast out demons requires the power of the Holy Spirit. Yet according to Jesus, having such power doesn't guarantee salvation.

So, just because the power of the Holy Spirit falls upon Cornelius and his Gentile companions prior to baptism and empowers them to speak in tongues, it doesn't *necessarily* follow that they were saved at that moment. Just as throughout salvation history God gave his Spirit for purposes besides salvation, it's possible that God gave his Spirit to Cornelius and his companions for some purpose besides salvation.

The context of the passage in question seems to suggest this. We're told that when the Holy Spirit fell upon Cornelius and the other Gentiles present, the "believers from among the circumcised who came with Peter were amazed, because the gift of the Holy Spirit had been poured out *even on the Gentiles*" (v. 45), the implication being that "believers from among the circumcised" initially *didn't* think this could happen. They knew that this had happened because "they heard them speaking in tongues and extolling God" (v. 46).

It seems that God gave his Spirit to convince the circumcised of what Peter had said at the outset of his speech in verse 34: that "God shows no partiality" and that "in every nation anyone who fears him and does what is right is acceptable to him." In other words, *because* of this visible manifestation of the Spirit, *all* can know that Cornelius and his Gentile friends can be saved. And it's on account of this that Peter is justified in giving such salvation to Cornelius and his Gentile friends through baptism.

Protestant author Everett Ferguson argues along these lines as well, writing,

> The baptism of the Holy Spirit in the case of Cornelius, instead of eliminating the need for water baptism, *was the justification administering it* (10:47–48). That Peter commanded water baptism shows the norm: If these Gentiles received the Holy Spirit, then they have to be baptized in water. The implication [Acts 11:17] is that God would have been hindered in giving salvation if they were denied baptism.[32]

On the interpretation that this event *is* an instance of salvation, which many have affirmed—like St. Thomas Aquinas[33]—receiving the Holy Spirit *before* baptism was fitting in *this* case, an *exceptional* case, given the need for a public demonstration of God's approval of the admission of Gentiles into the Church without the conditions of submitting to the Jewish ceremonial laws. Peter (Acts 10:9-16) and Cornelius (vv. 3-7) had both received private visions, but this occasion provided public evidence.[34]

The necessity of baptism, at least on the part of the Catholic Church, is not *absolute*. Catholic teaching allows for the belief that God can administer the graces of baptism without the sacrament. As the *Catechism* states, "God has bound salvation to the sacrament of baptism, but he himself is not bound by his sacraments" (1257). The event involving Cornelius and his Gentile friends could have been one of these cases where God acts without the sacrament.

But an exceptional case of God saving without baptism doesn't mean baptism isn't the ordinary means of salvation. Just as we'd say God can save someone living in a third-world jungle who has never heard of Jesus and thereby can't make an explicit act of faith, even though an explicit act of faith is an ordinary condition for receiving salvation, so too God can save Cornelius and his friends without baptism, even though baptism is the ordinary means of receiving the gift of salvation.

Todd Baker argues along the same lines as Rhodes.[35] Like Rhodes, he appeals to Acts 10:47-48. But Baker also appeals to several other New Testament passages to establish what he calls "the New Testament order for salvation," which, according to him, is "repentance, faith, and then water baptism."[36]

Baker cites several New Testament passages for support, including Acts 2:41, 8:12-13 and 36-38, and 9:18.[37] For Baker, these passages show that salvation is granted in response to faith. Therefore, he reasons, as soon as a person has faith, he's saved. And *this* is the ordinary pattern, so he claims. A believer doesn't need to wait for baptism, since, as Baker argues, "the rite of baptism does not precede the forgiveness of sins."

In all these passages, the faith that precedes baptism can be explained by what theologians call *imperfect* faith.[38] The assumption here is that the faith exercised before baptism in the passages cited is *perfect* faith, a faith animated by charity (Gal. 5:6) and that which justifies (Rom. 5:1). But that's not necessarily true. There is such a thing as *imperfect* faith that God gives to lead a person to and prepare him for the faith that justifies, which is given in baptism.

As St. Thomas Aquinas explains, faith, insofar as we distinguish it from hope and charity (1 Cor. 13:13), is an act of the intellect assenting to God's revelation by command of the will.[39] There is nothing in this understanding of faith that tells us whether charity informs it or not. There is nothing that tells us whether it's a faith that justifies or not, since charity is necessary for faith to justify.

God, nevertheless, gives this gift of faith to heal the person from unbelief. Belief in God's revelation, like repentance, is a necessary starting point for conversion (see Mark 1:15).

Evidence for such imperfect faith is found in the very event that both Rhodes and Baker appeal to for support of their claim: the reception of the Spirit by Cornelius and his Gentile friends in Acts 10. Before Cornelius is saved, whether through the reception of the Spirit (the view of most Christians) or through baptism (the view of a minority of Christians), Cornelius had faith.

For example, Luke tells us in verse 2 that Cornelius was a "devout man who *feared God*" and "prayed constantly to God." Then, in verse 4, we're told that Cornelius's prayers and alms "ascended as a memorial before God." In other words, his prayers were accepted. Surely, for Cornelius to fear God and have God accept his prayers implies that Cornelius had *some* form of faith. Yet this was *before* he was justified or saved.

Since there is a type of faith that exists without charity—a faith *prior* to salvation—Baker can't automatically conclude that the people who believed in the passages cited above were saved before baptism. Their belief that preceded their baptism could have been, and most likely was, that gift of faith not informed by charity, but which is necessary to cease in unbelief and then believe. Such faith would become perfect, or saving faith, upon receiving the virtue of charity that God grants in baptism. Therefore, the order found in the New Testament of repentance, belief, and baptism doesn't undermine the Catholic argument for the salvific value of baptism from Acts 2:38.

Pastoral Experience Suggests Regeneration Prior to Baptism

Now, a Protestant might adopt a counter like that of Gavin Ortlund, who says that according to his pastoral experience, this pattern of "salvation before baptism" seems to be the norm, for people who come to Christ manifest signs of regeneration prior to baptism.[40]

One response is that this comeback assumes that the person's belief in Jesus and change of lifestyle choices are *necessarily* a sign of regeneration. But such conversion experiences could be plausibly explained by the *imperfect* faith spoken of above, where the faith is not yet animated by charity. Thus, what one *thinks* are signs of regeneration might not be after all.

Secondly, as apologist Trent Horn points out,[41] Christians who believe in the "once saved, always saved" doctrine shouldn't be so quick to appeal to external signs as evidence for regeneration. Consider that most Christians who believe this doctrine also believe that if a Christian (who initially and for some time manifested "signs of regeneration") were to apostatize (deny Jesus) later in life, then such a person was never *really* a Christian to begin with—that's to say, he was never *really* saved.

But if this is true, then the initial and ongoing "signs of regeneration" weren't reliable for knowing whether the person was truly regenerate or not. This being the case, if a person manifests such "signs of regeneration" before baptism, we shouldn't automatically conclude that he is regenerated, nor should we appeal to them as evidence for the normal "order of salvation" to be regeneration before baptism.

Finally, this appeal to common pastoral experience just begs the question against believers in baptismal regeneration. Such experiences would be evidence against the causative nature of baptism *if and only if* we didn't have biblical data to support the claim that baptism saves. If the Bible reveals that God did establish baptism as the ordinary means of salvation, which we're arguing for in the current section of this book, then we would have reason to interpret these experiences to mean something else, whether we interpret them as cases of a person receiving spiritual gifts preceding salvation, such as imperfect faith (something for which there is biblical evidence—see Acts

10:2–4), or extraordinary cases of God regenerating without baptism (e.g., Acts 10:47–48).

Ultimately, the question becomes, "Should we filter our experiences through God's revelation, or should we filter God's revelation through our experiences?" I think most Christians would concede the latter: God's revelation must be the filter.

1 Peter 3:21

The next passage where Peter speaks of baptism is 1 Peter 3:21. He writes,

> God's patience waited in the days of Noah, during the building of the ark, in which a few, that is, eight persons, were saved through water. Baptism, which corresponds to this, now saves you, not as a removal of dirt from the body but as an appeal to God for a clear conscience, through the resurrection of Jesus Christ.

Peter can't be any clearer, Catholics (and the majority of other Christians) argue. He says, plain as day, "Baptism . . . now saves you." And Peter expounds the meaning of that salvation by telling us baptism brings about an interior cleansing inasmuch as it brings about a clear conscience. That implies that sins are forgiven, and the individual is saved.

But not all Christians accept this argument. Each comeback that we're going to consider here attempts to counter the argument from 1 Peter 3:21 by offering an alternative explanation as to what saves us.

What Saves Us Is Our Pledge to God to Follow Jesus

Some Protestants who deny the salvific efficacy of baptism argue that Peter isn't saying baptism actually saves us. Rather, it's the "appeal to God for a clear conscience," which is interpreted as a pledge to God to follow Jesus, that saves us, and baptism is merely an appropriate symbol for that confession of faith. Again, we look to Todd Baker for his articulation of the argument:

> Peter states in verse 21 that the real purpose of baptism is the "appeal" or "answer" of a good conscience toward God. The believer makes the pledge that he will now follow Jesus Christ as his obedient disciple united with the Lord in his death, burial, and resurrection.
>
> Baptism is an appropriate symbol of this reality for a public confession and act upon the one baptized openly declaring he or she now trusts in Jesus Christ for the forgiveness of sins with a pledge or an appeal to have a clear conscience now, cleansed from all guilt, condemnation, and accusation, that provides a good answer before God.[42]

The first thing to note is the interpretation of the phrase "an appeal to God for a clear conscience" as a *pledge* that we make to follow Jesus. This is important because if we were to translate it as an "appeal to God for a clear conscience," then Peter would be teaching us that we need to ask God to cleanse our conscience through baptism, which would support the idea that baptism saves. But if we're instructed to *pledge* a clear conscience to God, then the matter isn't as clear.

What should we make of this?

Well, there are a variety of opinions on how to read Peter's "*appeal* to God for a clear conscience." Some see this appeal as a "pledge" or "answer" with a good conscience to follow Jesus. The Protestant New International Version translation of the Bible renders the word as "pledge" rather than "appeal." This is not unreasonable, because the Greek word for "appeal," *eperotēma*, can mean "a pledge."[43] Others translate *eperotēma* as an "appeal," as the Revised Standard

Version does, the implication being that in baptism, Peter is saying we make a *request* of God to give us a clear, or good (1 Pet. 3:16), conscience. This is the primary meaning that many Greek dictionaries give for the word.[44]

Regardless of which translation we use for *eperotēma*, both correspond with the salvific efficacy of baptism. Take the view we're disputing right now, for example. The pledge to God to follow Christ with a good conscience doesn't preclude a sacramental understanding of baptism.

Christians who believe in the salvific efficacy of baptism profess that such a pledge to Christ is a necessary condition to receive baptism. (In the case of an infant, the parents and the Church make such a pledge on behalf of the child.) The pledge is part of the baptismal rite. And this pledge is made "with a good conscience," either because it's a sincere commitment or the person making the pledge in the baptismal rite is doing so having repented of sin, which is necessary to be baptized.

The view that translates *eperotēma* as "appeal" fits with the sacramental view of baptism as well. If we believe that God interiorly cleanses our souls by giving us a good conscience through the waters of baptism, then submitting ourselves to the baptismal waters is a request that God effect within our souls a clear, or good, conscience.

We can go further in our response to Baker. Consider that Peter's statement, "an appeal to God for a clear conscience," is one of two statements that Peter intends to explain what he means when he says, "Baptism now saves you." The other explanatory statement, which comes first and is set in opposition with the other, is "not as a removal of dirt from the body."

This creates a few problems for the interpretation that baptism *doesn't* save us and is *merely* a symbol of our pledge to follow Jesus. First, it's unreasonable to think Peter would make such an explicit statement about the salvific efficacy of baptism—"baptism now saves you"—and then immediately afterward deny such efficacy in his explanatory remarks.

Second, we end up having to think the language "as an appeal to God for a clear conscience" is meant to oppose the statement "baptism now saves us." But that's not what Peter says. Peter contrasts "as an appeal to God for a clear conscience" with the idea that baptism saves us "as a removal of dirt from the body."

This leads us to a third problem. It's true that Peter's denial of an external cleansing implies the affirmation of an internal cleansing: a "cleansing of guilt," as Rhodes puts it. But the argument runs off the rails by divorcing this internal cleansing from baptism, saying baptism is merely a symbol of the internal cleansing and is *not at all* an external cleansing. On the contrary, it's obvious that baptism *does* remove dirt from the body, so what Peter is denying is that baptism is *merely* "a removal of dirt from the body." It thus is *also* an internal cleansing.

It's Jesus' Resurrection that Saves, Not Baptism

Todd Baker puts the next comeback this way: "Peter tells his audience in verse 21 that it is the resurrection of Jesus Christ, symbolized by the waters of baptism, which actually saves the Christian."[45]

The main problem here is a false dichotomy: Our salvation is brought about *either* by Jesus' resurrection *or* by baptism. But if we consider Paul's teaching on baptism in Romans 6, we see that baptism is what allows us to *participate in* Jesus' resurrection, by which we are saved.

Paul introduces baptism in this chapter as the experience of death *and* resurrection in Christ:

> Do you not know that all of us who have been baptized into Christ Jesus were baptized into his death? We were buried therefore with him by baptism into death, so that as Christ was raised from the dead by the glory of the Father, we too might walk in newness of life (vv. 3-4).

Paul goes on to articulate the effects of this baptismal death and resurrection:

> We know that our old self was crucified with him so that the sinful body might be destroyed, and we might no longer be enslaved to sin. For he who has died is freed from sin (vv. 6-7).

As pointed out in the previous chapter, the Greek doesn't say "freed from sin." The Greek word translated "freed" is *dikaioō*, which means "to put into a right relationship (with God); acquit, declare and treat as righteous."[46] This is the same word Paul uses when he speaks of our justification by faith: "Since we are justified [Greek, *dikaiōthentes*] by faith, we have peace with God through our Lord Jesus Christ" (Rom. 5:1). So the phrase "freed from sin" in Romans 6:7 can literally be translated "justified from sin."

Modern translations render it as "freed from sin" because the context is clearly about sanctification. For example, in the verse before Paul speaks of baptismal death, he speaks of those in Christ as having "died to sin." As quoted above, Paul speaks of those who have died the death of baptism as "no longer enslaved to sin."

This tells us that for Paul, justification can include sanctification, which is the interior renewal of the soul whereby the objective guilt of sin is removed. And that justification, or salvation, takes place in baptism.

A third problem with the "Resurrection" counterargument is that it contradicts the plain sense of the text: "Baptism now saves you." Peter doesn't say, "The Resurrection saves you." It would have been unnatural for Peter to use the language "baptism now saves you" in order to convey the message "baptism *doesn't* save you; Christ's resurrection does."

Conclusion

So far, we've appealed to the source himself of divine revelation, Jesus, for evidence that baptism saves. We've also appealed to what the two greatest apostles—Peter and Paul—have to say about baptism. Our next order of business is to look at what *other* Christians believed about baptism and see whether their belief fits the belief we've been advocating for so far in this book.

Chapter 4

The Early Church Says So

Technically, our appeal to St. Paul and St. Peter in the previous two chapters would fit under this category—that is, what the early Church says about baptism. However, given their unique status as apostles and the priority of their teaching, I judged it fitting to devote a chapter to each.

We will begin this chapter in the first century, with Ananias, and then work our way through the fourth century to Cyril of Jerusalem. We will also consider a counterargument from the Fathers on this issue toward the end of the chapter.

Ananias (Acts 22:16)

Our first witness for the early Church is the first-century Christian Ananias, the one whom the Lord instructed in a vision to meet the newly converted Saul and lay hands on him that he might regain his sight (Acts 9:10-12). When Paul describes this encounter with Ananias in Acts 22, he recounts what Ananias told him:

> The God of our fathers appointed you to know his will, to see the Just One and to hear a voice from his mouth; for you will be a witness for him to all men of what you have seen and heard. And now why do you wait? Rise and *be baptized, and wash away your sins*, calling on his name (vv. 14-16).

Notice what Ananias *doesn't* say: "Rise and be baptized, *because* you've been forgiven your sins." Rather, his instruction implies that baptism will *bring about* the forgiveness of Saul's sins, which, as mentioned above, is to interpret this command in the "causal sense."

Moreover, and more importantly, the verb in the above passage, "wash away," clearly connects baptism with sins. This reveals that baptism *is* a washing. The statement "be baptized and wash away your sins" depicts the *washing* of baptism as what *removes* the sins.

Now, our Protestant friends aren't short of comebacks to this line of reasoning. So let's consider whether they have any persuasive force.

Paul Was Already Saved

One possible counterargument is that Paul was already saved since he received the Holy Spirit *before* his baptism. Like in the counterargument above, reception of the Holy Spirit is often equated with salvation (cf. Rom. 8:9). Gavin Ortlund makes this argument in his online video, "Baptismal Regeneration: Responding to Common Arguments," although he doesn't make it as a counter to Acts 22:16. Rather, he makes the argument in support of the general theme mentioned above that the New Testament pattern for salvation is salvation before baptism.[47] But this argument *could* be used as a comeback to the above exegesis of Acts 22:16. Here's Ortlund's commentary on the exchange between Ananias and Saul:

> Even with Paul in Acts chapter nine when Ananias lays hands on Paul, the Spirit descends upon him upon the laying on of Ananias's hands, and he receives his sight back at that time according to Acts 9:17-18. And then

> subsequently he rises up and is baptized. That's not instrumental means of regeneration.[48]

One problem with Ortlund's argument is that he reads into the text (Acts 9:17-18) something that's not there. Notice that he states, "The Spirit descends upon [Paul] *upon the laying on of Ananias's hands.*" But that's not what Luke records. Here's the actual text: "And laying his hands on [Saul] he said, 'Brother Saul the Lord Jesus who appeared to you on the road by which you came, has sent me that you may regain your sight and be filled with the Holy Spirit'" (Acts 9:17).

Notice that the phrase "be filled with the Holy Spirit" isn't specifying what happens when Ananias lays his hands on Saul. Rather, it's specifying the *purpose* for which the Lord sent Ananias—namely, to give Saul the Holy Spirit, along with his sight. As to *when* the Holy Spirit is to be given, Ananias doesn't say. It *could* be at the time Ananias is saying the words, or it *could* very well be when Saul is baptized. Other evidence would have to be provided to discern *when* the Spirit is given. Given such ambiguity, Ortlund, or any Christian who rejects baptismal regeneration, can't appeal to this text as evidence for the New Testament pattern of "salvation before baptism." Nor can it be used as a counterargument against the above exegesis of Acts 22:16.

Now, Ortlund might respond that perhaps the text doesn't explicitly say the Spirit is given at the time Ananias lays his hands on Saul. But this is a reasonable assumption, given the fact that elsewhere in Scripture, the Spirit *is* given at the time someone has their hands laid on them. For example, in Acts 8:17, the Spirit was given through the laying on of hands (by Peter and John) to new believers in Samaria. Given this biblical precedent, it's reasonable to assume that Saul receives the Spirit *when* Ananias lays his hands on him.

The problem here is that the Samarians in Acts 8 had already been baptized when they received the laying on of hands, whereas Saul had not. Given the two different scenarios, a Christian can't use the laying on of hands in Acts 8 as an interpretative context for the laying on of hands in Acts 9, especially when Luke explicitly specifies that the Holy Spirit *is* given through the laying on of hands in Acts 8 ("Then they laid their hands on them and they received the Holy Spirit. Now when Simon saw that the Spirit was given *through the laying on of the apostles' hands*, he offered them money"—vv. 17-18), but doesn't make such a specification in Acts 9, saying only that Ananias was sent *to give* the Spirit to Saul. Perhaps Luke lacks such specification because he believed that the Spirit was to be given when Saul was baptized. That would fit the biblical data that we've presented so far in this book.

A second problem with Ortlund's above argument is that he assumes that the giving of the Spirit equals salvation. But, as mentioned above, being filled with the Holy Spirit doesn't necessarily entail salvation. The Spirit can be given for purposes other than salvation.

Assuming Saul *did* receive the Spirit when Ananias laid his hands on him, it could be that Saul received the Holy Spirit for miraculous purposes—for the sake of being healed of his blindness. This would fit the immediate context, since right after the laying on of hands, we're told that Saul receives his sight back: "And immediately something like scales fell from his eyes and he regained his sight" (v. 18). So Saul could very well have received the Holy Spirit before he was baptized, but that wouldn't necessarily mean he was saved before baptism.

Now, a Christian might respond that there are other details besides the giving of the Spirit that suggest Paul was already saved. Baker takes this route specifically and appeals to two such details, both of which are affirmed of Paul *before* he was baptized: 1) Paul was called a "chosen vessel" (Acts 9:15), and 2) Ananias calls Saul "brother."[49]

Concerning the "chosen vessel" bit, Baker would have us think the meaning of Saul's election is restricted to being saved. But the text cited by Baker proves that this is *not* the case. Here's how Acts 9:15 actually reads: "The Lord said to [Ananias], 'Go, for he [Saul] is a chosen instrument of mine to carry my name before the Gentiles and kings and the sons of Israel.'" The purpose of the election is for the sake of evangelization. Saul's salvation, surely, is part of God's predestined plan, but that doesn't mean Saul was saved the moment God told Ananias that Saul was "chosen" to carry out God's message to the nations.

What about Ananias calling Saul "brother"? Well, Baker assumes that for Ananias to call Saul "brother," it must mean that Saul is already in Christ, as if that's the only possible interpretation. But this is not true. It's possible that Ananias calls Saul "brother" to signify Saul as a fellow Jew.

Luke tells us that Ananias was "a devout observer of the law and highly respected by all the Jews living there" (Acts 22:12). And we know that Jews referred to fellow Jews as "brother." For example, Paul calls his "kinsmen according to the flesh"—Jews—"my brethren" (Rom. 9:3).

Thus, Baker's view that Saul is already saved is not the only plausible explanation for why Ananias calls him "brother."

Furthermore, this interpretation, that Ananias was saluting a fellow Jew, is even more likely, given that Ananias's instruction implies that Saul's sins had not been washed away yet (Acts 22:16). How can you be in Christ—saved—without first having all your sins washed away?

So Ananias's mere use of "brother" *also* doesn't necessarily entail that Saul was already a Christian, and thus already saved before baptism. Both of Baker's details fail to prove his thesis that Paul was *already* saved.

Paul Was Saved by Calling on the Lord's Name

Baker has yet another comeback in his back pocket. He argues that Paul wasn't saved by baptism. Rather, he was saved by calling on the name of the Lord. He writes,

> The Greek text of Acts 22:16, where the verbs "be baptized" (βαπτισαι) and "wash away" (απόλουσαι) occur, are both in the aorist imperative tense and are commands, while "arise" (αναστας) and "calling" (ἐπικαλεσάμενος) are participle verbs in the aorist tense. Taking all this into consideration, based on the grammatical construction of the original Greek text, the passage can literally be translated to read: "Having arisen be baptized, and have your sins washed (by) calling on the name of the Lord."
>
> It was by the calling on the name of the Lord, that Saul's sins would be washed away. The washing away of sins is directly associated with calling on the name of the Lord, not with baptism. This is exactly what the Bible teaches (see Isa. 55:1; Jer. 33:3; Joel 2:32; Acts 2:21), and it is what Paul also taught and wrote in Romans 10:13—"Whoever calls upon the name of the Lord will be saved." The forgiveness of sins in Paul's case, and in the case of all believers, occurs when they call upon the Lord for salvation; the waters of baptism do not magically produce it.
>
> The baptism of Paul was a figurative gesture that pictures what had occurred in his inner life—his soul and heart were transformed and the guilt of his sin washed away by the forgiveness of Christ. Baptism is "a picture of God's inner work of washing away sin" (1 Cor. 6:11; 1 Pet. 3:21).[50]

One problem with Baker's exegesis here is that he contradicts what he said earlier. Here he says Saul was saved by "calling on the name of the Lord." Yet in the previous sentences of the same paragraph, Baker argues that Paul "*had already experienced salvation* when he was personally confronted, touched, and commissioned by the risen Christ on the road to Damascus three days earlier before the events with Ananias and baptism (Acts 9:9–17; 26:15–18; Gal. 1:12)."[51] He goes on to further cite the above details of Saul being called a "chosen vessel" and "brother." All of this occurred *before* Ananias tells Saul to "call on the name of the Lord." So Baker seems a bit confused himself as to when Saul was saved.

But that aside, there's a second problem. Notice that Baker inserts the preposition "by" within his quotation of the text to indicate that Saul's calling on the Lord's name is the *cause* of him having his sins forgiven. He does this to try to capture the meaning of the aorist participle—"calling," which "usually refers to antecedent time with respect to the main verb,"[52] which in this case is "wash." In Baker's mind, since the Greek suggests that "calling on the name of the Lord" comes *before* Saul has his sins washed away, calling on the Lord's name must thereby be the *cause* of such an effect.

We have no qualms with Baker here. But where he goes wrong is his *either-or* paradigm. For Baker, it's *either* calling on the Lord's name that brings about the forgiveness of sins *or* baptism. But that just begs the question against the believer in baptismal regeneration, since if baptism does indeed bring about the forgiveness of sins, then it would be *both* calling on the Lord's name *and* baptism through which Saul would have his sins forgiven. And that's exactly what believers in baptismal regeneration believe happens in the rite of baptism. Calling on the Lord's name through the profession of faith *accompanies* the ritual washing. It's a both-and thing, not either-or.

St. Ignatius of Antioch

Our next witness to early Christian belief in baptismal regeneration is Ignatius of Antioch. In his Letter to the Trallians (A.D. 110), he echoes Paul's teaching from Romans 6:4 that through baptism we rise to a "newness of life." He writes,

> Wherefore also, ye appear to me to live not after the manner of men, but according to Jesus Christ, who died for us, in order that, by believing in his death, ye may *by baptism be made partakers of his resurrection.*[53]

To be made partakers of Christ's resurrection is to experience a spiritual resurrection, which necessarily implies a prior state of spiritual death. But passage from spiritual death to spiritual life is the essence of salvation. For Ignatius, therefore, baptism saves, since it's through baptism that we spiritually rise in Christ.

In the above quotation, Ignatius echoes Paul's teaching in Romans 6:4 that we rise with Christ in baptism. In his Letter to the Philippians, Ignatius emphasizes the other side of Paul's coin: death in baptism. Paul writes, "Do you not know that all of us who have been baptized into Christ Jesus were baptized into his death?" (Rom. 6:3). Here's what Ignatius writes:

> And also one baptism, which is administered that we should have fellowship with the death of the Lord; and also one elect Church; there ought likewise to be but one faith in respect to Christ.[54]

To have fellowship with the death of the Lord means to participate in Christ's passion, which means to assimilate the fruits of the cross—namely, salvation. Since Ignatius believes that baptism incorporates us into Christ's death, it follows that Ignatius believes that baptism saves.

Letter of Barnabas

The Letter of Barnabas, an early Christian document that dates anywhere from A.D. 70 to 135,[55] also witnesses to the salvific efficacy of baptism. It does so by emphasizing the forgiveness of sins brought about through baptism. Here's the relevant text:

> We descend into the water full of sins and defilement, but come up bearing fruit in our heart, having the fear of God and trust in Jesus in our spirit (11).

Not only does this passage confirm belief in the forgiveness of sins in baptism, but it also indirectly hints at the inner renewal, or the new birth, that is brought about, since it speaks of fruit borne *in the heart*, having "the fear of God and trust in Jesus."

The Shepherd of Hermas

Next up we have the Shepherd of Hermas, also known as "The Shepherd," which dates no later than A.D. 145. (Some even put it as early as A.D. 80.[56]) In chapter three of the fourth commandment in book two, Hermas asks the messenger whether it is true that there is "no other repentance than that which takes place, when [they] descended into the water and received remission of [their] former sins."[57] The messenger responds, "That was sound doctrine which you heard."

Then, later in The Shepherd, the messenger instructs Hermas with an allusion to Paul's teaching in Romans 6:3-4, stating,

> They were obliged to ascend through water in order that they might be made alive; for, unless they laid aside the deadness of their life, they could not in any other way enter into the kingdom of God. Accordingly, those also who fell asleep received the seal of the Son of God. For

> before a man bears the name of the Son of God he is dead; but when he receives the seal he lays aside his deadness, and obtains life. The seal, then, is the water: they descend into the water dead, and they arise alive. And to them, accordingly, was this seal preached, and they made use of it that they might enter into the kingdom of God.[58]

According to the above teachings from the messenger, three things happen in baptism:

1. forgiveness of sins,
2. transference from spiritual death to spiritual life, and
3. entrance into the kingdom of God.

If that's not salvation, then nothing is. And for this messenger, this all happens in water baptism. Water baptism, therefore, was believed at this time to be salvific, *not* merely a symbol.

St. Justin Martyr

Next up among our early witnesses to the salvific efficacy of baptism is Justin Martyr, a second-century Christian convert and apologist. In his *First Apology* (A.D. 150), chapter sixty-one, Justin gives a teaching as to "the manner in which [believers are] dedicated . . . to God when [they] had been made new through Christ."[59] He writes,

> As many as are persuaded and believe that what we teach and say is true, and undertake to be able to live accordingly, are instructed to pray and to entreat God with fasting, for the remission of their sins that are past, we praying and fasting with them. Then they are brought by us where there is water, and *are regenerated in the same manner in which we were ourselves regenerated.*

> For, in the name of God, the Father and Lord of the universe, and of our Savior Jesus Christ, and of the Holy Spirit, they then receive the washing with water. For Christ also said, "Except ye be born again, ye shall not enter into the kingdom of heaven.[60]

Notice that Justin interprets Jesus' "born again" teaching as a reference to baptism. And for Justin, such regeneration involved *the remission of sins*. Consider what he writes next:

> And for this [rite] we have learned from the apostles this reason. Since at our birth we were born without our own knowledge or choice, by our parents coming together, and were brought up in bad habits and wicked training; in order that we may not remain the children of necessity and of ignorance, but may become the children of choice and knowledge, and *may obtain in the water the remission of sins formerly committed*, there is pronounced over him who chooses to be born again, and has repented of his sins, the name of God the Father and Lord of the universe.[61]

If baptism regenerates by way of remitting sins, then it follows that baptism saves, since such regeneration and remission of sins is what salvation is. Justin believes that baptism regenerates by way of remitting sins. Therefore, Justin believes that baptism saves.

Some Christians might not be so easily convinced. For example, Ortlund counters that Justin uses the term "baptism," along with terms like "washing" and "bath," as a *metonymy*—that is, a figure of speech whereby a concept is referred to by the name of something closely associated with that concept—"for the entire process"[62] of things leading up to baptism. Because of this, Ortlund concludes that just because a Church Father speaks of "baptism" as regenerating someone, it doesn't necessarily follow that the actual rite of water baptism is a cause of salvation. Here's the relevant quote from Justin:

> By reason, therefore, of this *laver of repentance and knowledge of God*, which has been ordained on account of the transgression of God's people, as Isaiah cries, we have believed, and testify that *that very baptism which he announced* is alone *able to purify* those who have repented; and *this is the water of life*. . . .
>
> For what is the use of that baptism which cleanses the flesh and body alone? *Baptize the soul* from wrath and from covetousness, from envy, and from hatred.[63]

Notice that Justin speaks of "repentance" and "knowledge of God" as the "laver" (or washing), "the water of life," and "baptism." He even juxtaposes a baptism that cleanses the body and a baptism that cleanses the soul. It would seem, therefore, that Justin doesn't think the rite of baptism actually brings about salvation. Rather, it's repentance. As Ortlund states, "what's the baptism that cleanses the soul? Repentance. You repent, and *that* baptizes your soul."[64] And such repentance is called "baptism" because baptism is closely associated with repentance insofar as baptism is the sign of repentance.

The first thing we can say in response is that Ortlund simply *assumes* a particular directionality in the metonymy. He reasons that the actions preceding the rite of baptism are in fact the actions that save us, and they are *spoken* of as "baptism" because of their close association to the actual rite of baptism.

However, the reverse could just as easily be true. It could very well be that Justin *speaks* of the preceding actions as saving actions because of their close association to the in fact saving action of baptism. In other words, it could be that Justin speaks of the things that precede baptism—namely, "repentance" and "knowledge of God"—as "purifying" us and saving us because they lead to, and are necessary conditions for, using the instrument that in fact saves: baptism.

This reading isn't merely hypothetical. It seems to be the more probable reading. One reason is that Justin says in the two passages initially quoted above that baptism regenerates us by way of remitting our sins. This means he believes that baptism is that which in fact saves us, at least in an instrumental way.

Another factor that supports this reading is that Justin explicitly teaches that the ritual washing *by itself* cannot save. Note the quote from above: "For what is the use of that baptism which cleanses the flesh and body alone?" Justin's point is that the ritual washing itself is ineffective for our salvation. Repentance, at least for adults, must *accompany* such a washing. This is why he says, "Baptize *the soul* from wrath and from covetousness, from envy, and from hatred." A mere ritual washing isn't going to do anything. There must be a corresponding *spiritual conformity* to what the washing signifies; otherwise, it's futile.

But just because repentance must accompany the ritual washing for us to be saved that doesn't mean the repentance by itself—*without* the washing—is what in fact saves. Repentance is the *necessary prerequisite* for the ritual washing, and both *together* bring about our salvation. As Jesus teaches in Mark 16:16, "he who believes [also repents] and is baptized will be saved." Given that repentance is a necessary prerequisite for the ritual washing through which we are saved—i.e., baptism—it makes sense that Justin would use a metonymy and speak of such repentance as being the "baptism" that saves us.

So Justin Martyr can still be a witness for the early Christian belief that baptism is an instrumental cause of regeneration, or salvation.

St. Irenaeus of Lyon

We now move forward in our survey about thirty or so years to Irenaeus, who was the bishop of Lyon, France from around A.D. 178 to his death in 200. Like Justin, Irenaeus believed that baptism regenerates. He expresses this belief in a few of his works. One is his *Against Heresies* (A.D. 189). In commenting on Christ's commission for the apostles to go into all nations and make disciples by baptizing them (Matt. 28:19), Irenaeus teaches that Christ gave his apostles the "power of regeneration into God."[65]

He goes on to affirm that by the "water from heaven" believers are "made one in Christ Jesus."[66] According to Romans 8:1, to be in Christ is to not be subject to condemnation, which means to be saved. Baptism, therefore, at least for Irenaeus, saves.

But for Irenaeus, it's not just the ritual water that brings about regeneration and puts us in Christ. Rather, water *together with the Spirit* brings it about, which, of course, alludes to Jesus' teaching of regeneration by water *and* the Spirit in John 3:5. Irenaeus writes,

> And as dry earth does not bring forth unless it receive moisture, in like manner we also, being originally a dry tree, could never have brought forth fruit unto life without the voluntary rain from above. For our bodies have received unity among themselves by *means of that laver* which leads to incorruption; but our souls, *by means of the Spirit*. Wherefore both are necessary, since *both contribute toward the life of God*.[67]

Notice that *both* water and the Spirit are necessary for the believer to receive "the life of God"—i.e., to be regenerated. As we argued in our exegesis of the Born Again discourse, *both* water *and* Spirit constitute the second birth.

In the above quotes, Irenaeus affirms that regeneration happens in baptism and that the "life of God" is given, but noticeably, he doesn't say anything about the remission of sins. Does he conceive of this regeneration as something else besides the transference from interior defilement to righteousness? No, he doesn't. He affirms the remission of sins as being involved in the baptismal regeneration in his work *On the Apostolic Teaching* (c. A.D. 180–190). Here's the relevant text:

> So faith procures this for us, as the elders, the disciples of the apostles, have handed down to us: Firstly, *it exhorts us to remember that we have received baptism for the remission of sins*, in the name of God the Father, and in the name of Jesus Christ, the Son of God, [who was] incarnate, and died, and was raised, and in the Holy Spirit of God; and that *this baptism is the seal of eternal life and rebirth unto God, that we may no longer be sons of mortal men, but of the eternal and everlasting God.*[68]

In a later section, he describes this remission as a "cleansing," writing,

> The apostles, who being sent by him, with the power of the Holy Spirit, into the whole world, realized the call of the Gentiles, showing mankind the way of life, turning them away from idols and from fornication and from avarice, *cleansing their souls and bodies by the baptism of water and the Holy Spirit*, distributing and dispensing the Holy Spirit, which they received from the Lord, to the faithful—and in this way they established the churches.[69]

So, like those before him, Irenaeus believes that baptism is a means of salvation.

St. Clement of Alexandria

The last major witness of the second century is St. Clement of Alexandria. Clement is big on the illuminating aspect of baptism. But within the context of his explanation of the illumination that takes place, he affirms the remission of sins in baptism, along with a change of the interior quality of the soul. The quote is a bit lengthy but worth presenting in some detail. In his *Instructor* (A.D. 198), he writes,

> Being baptized, we are illuminated; illuminated, we become sons; being made sons, *we are made perfect*; being made perfect, we are made immortal. . . .
>
> This work is variously called grace, and illumination, and perfection, and washing: *washing, by which we cleanse away our sins*; grace, by which the penalties accruing to transgressions are remitted; and illumination, by which that holy light of salvation is beheld—that is, by which we see God clearly.
>
> Now we call that perfect which wants nothing. For what is yet wanting to him who knows God? . . . We who are baptized, *having wiped off the sins* which obscure the light of the Divine Spirit, have the eye of the spirit free, unimpeded, and full of light, by which alone we contemplate the divine, the Holy Spirit flowing down to us from above. . . .
>
> For what ignorance has bound ill, is by knowledge loosed well; those bonds are with all speed slackened by human faith and divine grace, *our transgressions being taken away* by one Paeonian medicine [referring to *Paeon* or *Paean*, a name applied in Greek mythology to the divine

> healer Apollo], the baptism of the Word. *We are washed from all our sins*, and are no longer entangled in evil. This is the one grace of illumination, *that our characters are not the same as before our washing. . . .*
>
> In the same way, therefore, we also, repenting of our sins, renouncing our iniquities, *purified by baptism*, speed back to the eternal light, children to the Father.[70]

As we've argued above, to speak of the remission of sins and our interior character being purified is to speak of salvation. Since Clement believes that baptism brings this about, it follows that he believes that baptism saves.

Tertullian

We now move in our survey to the third century. One theologian we can appeal to for our purposes is Tertullian, a prolific Christian author from Carthage, in the Roman province of Africa. In his work *On Baptism* (203), he makes explicit the belief that salvation is brought about through baptism, and he supports such a belief with Jesus' Born Again discourse. He writes,

> When the prescript is laid down that "*without baptism, salvation is attainable by none*" (chiefly on the ground of that declaration of the Lord, who says, "Unless one be born of water, he hath not life" [John 3:5]), there arise immediately scrupulous, nay rather audacious, doubts on the part of some—"How, in accordance with that prescript, salvation is attainable by the apostles, whom—Paul excepted—we do not find baptized in the Lord?"[71]

Tertullian goes on to argue, contra his interlocutors, why he thinks the apostles were indeed baptized, despite there being no explicit evidence in the New Testament. Even if they weren't, that would not disprove the salvific efficacy of baptism, since, as we've argued above, God can give the grace of salvation apart from the sacrament. Regardless, it's clear that Tertullian believed that baptism saves. And he believes that it is revealed by our Lord himself.

St. Hippolytus

Hippolytus of Rome is another third-century prolific theologian who affirms the regenerative nature of baptism. However, he probes a bit deeper than the previous theologians cited by identifying *divinization* as an effect of baptism—where the baptized participates in the divine life. Here's what he writes in his Discourse on the Holy Theophany (217):

> The Father of immortality sent the immortal Son and Word into the world, who came to man in order to wash him *with water and the Spirit; and he, begetting us again to incorruption of soul and body, breathed into us the Spirit of life,* and endued us with an incorruptible panoply.
>
> If, therefore, man has become immortal, *he will also be God.* And if he is made God by water and the Holy Spirit after the regeneration of the laver he is found to be also joint-heir with Christ after the resurrection from the dead. Wherefore I preach to this effect: Come, all ye kindreds of the nations, to the immortality of the baptism.[72]

The affirmation that the baptized "becomes God" is to be understood in the sense of *participating* in the divine nature. As St. Peter writes, "[Christ] has granted to us his precious and very great promises, that through these you may escape from the corruption that is in the world because of passion, and become *partakers of the divine nature*" (2 Pet. 1:4).

This is precisely how the *Catechism of the Catholic Church* interprets this language, citing 2 Peter 1:4, when it explains the meaning of the language as used by St. Athanasius in his *On the Incarnation of the Word* ("For the Son of God became man so that we might become God"[73]). Such participation in the divine life is nothing other than salvation. Since Hippolytus believes that baptism brings about such participation, it follows that Hippolytus believes that baptism saves.

St. John Chrysostom

We now move in our survey to the fourth century. Two Fathers who exemplify the fourth-century belief in the salvific efficacy of baptism are St. John Chrysostom and St. Cyril of Jerusalem.

Let's start with John Chrysostom. The quote below primarily focuses on infant baptism and the reasons why Christians practice it. However, the reasons he lists shed light on what Christians at this period believed about baptism. Here's his teaching as recorded in the Baptismal Catecheses in Augustine, *Against Julian*:

> You see how many are the benefits of baptism, and some think its heavenly grace consists only in *the remission of sins*, but we have enumerated ten honors [it bestows]! For this reason we baptize even infants, though they are not defiled by [personal] sins, so that there may be given to them *holiness, righteousness, adoption, inheritance, brotherhood with Christ*, and that they *may be [Christ's] members*.[74]

Like the Fathers before him, Chrysostom affirms that baptism remits sins, at least for those who have such sins to be remitted, such as adults. But he penetrates the mystery by saying baptism is the instrument through which the infant is made *holy* and *righteous*. And not only does the infant become holy, but he is *adopted as a child of God*, receiving the *inheritance* of eternal life.

St. Cyril of Jerusalem

Cyril's understanding of baptism is manifest in lecture three of his Catechetical Lectures. The first quote is explicit that he believes that baptism saves. He writes,

> If any man receive not baptism, *he hath not salvation*; except only martyrs, who even without the water receive the kingdom. For when the Savior, in redeeming the world by his cross, was pierced in the side, he shed forth blood and water; that men, living in times of peace, might be baptized in water, and, in times of persecution, in their own blood.[75]

What's interesting here is that there is no ambiguity as to the nature of "salvation" that Cyril has in mind. The salvation that a martyr receives through the "baptism of blood" is the same salvation that one receives through the "baptism of water."

Cyril then roots the above claim in St. Paul's theology of baptism, as articulated in Romans 6:3-4:

> For you go down into the water, bearing your sins, but the invocation of grace, having sealed your soul, *suffers you not afterwards to be swallowed up by the terrible dragon.* Having gone down dead in sins, you *come up quickened in righteousness.*
>
> For if you have been united with the likeness of the Savior's death, you shall also be deemed worthy of his resurrection. For as Jesus took upon him the sins of the world, and died, that by putting sin to death he might rise again in righteousness; so you by going down into the water, and being in a manner buried in the waters, as he was in the rock, art *raised again walking in newness of life.*[76]

Notice that for Cyril, not only does baptism save in the sense of not being under the dominion of Satan ("suffers you not afterwards to be swallowed up by the terrible dragon"), but it makes one *righteous* ("you come up quickened in righteousness). This tracks with Paul's theology in Romans 6:7 that those who die the baptismal death are "*justified* from sin" (see chapter two).

Moreover, Cyril alludes to Paul's teaching on baptismal death and resurrection in Romans 6:3-4. For Cyril, like Paul, we are united to Christ's death in baptism and consequently are also united to Christ's resurrection, such that through baptism we rise to a "newness of life." Like those before him, Cyril believes that baptism saves.

Now, in his YouTube video "Baptismal Regeneration: Responding to Common Arguments," Gavin Ortlund counters by appealing to Cyril's comments (from the same lecture above—lecture three) on Cornelius, where Cyril affirms that Cornelius was regenerated *prior* to receiving baptism. Here's Cyril's quote:

> Cornelius was a just man, who was honored with a vision of angels, and had set up his prayers and alms-deeds as a good memorial before God in heaven.
>
> Peter came, and the Spirit was poured out upon them that believed, and they spoke with other tongues, and prophesied: and after the grace of the Spirit the Scripture says that Peter commanded them to be baptized in the name of Jesus Christ; in order that, the *soul* having been *born again by faith*, the *body* also might by the water partake of the *grace*.[77]

For Ortlund, this is evidence that Cyril "coordinated faith and baptism together . . . seeing them, like, as two parts of one thing," where "baptism and salvation can have this profound relationship without being a causative one."[78] How might we respond?

First, we *could* say, "Wait a minute! The two quotes above from lecture three prove that Cyril believed in baptismal regeneration. How can Ortlund say Cyril didn't believe baptism is causative of salvation?" But Ortlund has a response. In the same video, he pre-empts such an objection, stating,

> People are going to go nuts and come up with all these other quotes in Cyril. I've read through the Catechetical Lectures very carefully. I'm aware there's other passages where he talks about baptism in a very high way. My point is, he does understand Cornelius to have been born again at the moment of faith, and yet he still speaks of baptism as regenerative for him.[79]

Does Ortlund's counter block our initial response? No, it doesn't!

The problem with Ortlund's counterargument is that he leads the listener to think Cyril only "*speaks* of baptism as regenerative," the assumption being that such vague speech would allow for further specification that baptism and regeneration by faith are related, but not in a causal way. But this is not the case.

As the first quote from above shows, Cyril believes that the relationship between baptism and salvation is parallel to the relationship between salvation and martyrdom. Just as martyrdom brings about salvation for a believer, so too does baptism. If we were to follow Ortlund's logic, we'd have to say Cyril doesn't believe that martyrdom is in some way causative of salvation. But that contradicts the explicit meaning of the text.

In the second quote, Cyril makes it clear that *through* baptism someone is made holy and righteous and is raised to a new life. If being made holy and righteous is what salvation means, which seems to be the case for Cyril, since he believes that such a new state protects one from the "dragon" (Satan), then Cyril believes that a believer is saved *through* baptism. This seems to be not at all different from the expressed teaching of the Council of Trent that baptism is the "instrumental cause" of salvation.[80]

A second response is that Cyril doesn't appeal to the event of Cornelius to prove that baptism isn't causative of regeneration. Rather, Cyril appeals to the event simply to prove the necessity of having *both* water *and* Spirit for "salvation" and being "made perfect," which for Cyril follows from man's "twofold nature, soul and body."[81]

That Cornelius's spirit is regenerated apart from the ritual washing in this special case doesn't mean that *everyone*'s spirit is regenerated by faith before baptism. Again, Cyril makes clear in the first two quotes above that he believes that baptism is the instrumental cause of salvation, which means ordinarily spiritual regeneration and ritual washing happen simultaneously.

Universal Consent

The survey of early Christians that we've considered in this chapter is obviously limited. However, it's exemplary of what the early Church believed by way of *universal consent*. Even Protestant scholarship confirms this.

For example, J.N.D. Kelly, an Anglican Patristic scholar, writes, "From the beginning baptism was the universally accepted rite of admission to the Church. . . . As regards its significance, it was *always* held to convey the remission of sins."[82] William Webster concurs: "The doctrine of baptism is one of the few teachings within Roman Catholicism for which it can be said that there is a universal consent of the Fathers."[83]

According to Pope Leo XIII's 1893 encyclical letter *Providentissimus Deus* (Most Provident God), and its teaching on the unanimous consent of the early Church Fathers on a particular doctrine, it would seem that the salvific efficacy of baptism is part and parcel of the Faith that the apostles handed down. Leo states,

> The Holy Fathers, we say, are of supreme authority, whenever they all interpret in one and the same manner any text of the Bible, as pertaining to the doctrine of faith or morals; for their unanimity clearly evinces that such interpretation has come down from the apostles *as a matter of Catholic faith*. The opinion of the Fathers is also of very great weight when they treat of these matters in their capacity of doctors, unofficially.[84]

To speak of a teaching as being "a matter of Catholic faith" is technical terminology in Catholic theology to indicate that something is an infallibly defined teaching that's part of divine revelation.[85] As argued for above, the salvific efficacy of baptism is unanimous among the early Church Fathers. Therefore, according to Leo XIII, such a teaching is part of divine revelation and thereby necessary to believe for salvation.

CHAPTER 5

The Magisterium Says So

So far in this book, we've looked at what Jesus says concerning the relation between baptism and salvation. We've also looked at what Christians have had to say on the matter. Ss. Peter and Paul are representative of what the apostles taught. And we surveyed Christians from the first three centuries to see what they believed was part of what the apostles handed on to them. What's left now is a survey of what the Magisterium has taught throughout the centuries.

Fifteenth (or Sixteenth) Council of Carthage (418)[86]

Let's start in the fifth century with the Fifteenth Council of Carthage (418). Even though it's a local council and not ecumenical, it still retains the status of magisterial teaching. Its teaching on the salvific efficacy of baptism comes about within the context of the question of whether infants should be baptized. The council answers in the affirmative. The reasons for this answer illustrate what the Church believed about baptism. Canon 2 is the relevant canon, which comes among others concerning original sin and grace:

> It has been decided: whoever says that little children right from their mothers' wombs ought not to be baptized or says that they are indeed baptized for the forgiveness of sins but that they derive from Adam no trace of original

> sin that would have to be removed by *the bath of rebirth*, when it follows that in their case the baptismal formula "*for the remission of sins*" is to be understood as not true but false, let him be anathema.
>
> For in no other way must one understand that which the apostle says: "Through one man sin entered into the world (and through sin, death), and so it has passed on into all men; in him all have sinned" (cf. Rom. 5:12) except as the Catholic Church spread throughout the world has always understood it. For because of this tenet of the faith even little children, who in themselves have not yet been able to commit any sins, are in consequence baptized truly for the remission of sins, so that in them that which was incurred by their birth may be *cleansed by their rebirth*.[87]

For the council fathers, baptism rids the infant of original sin and regenerates him. To say otherwise is to be excluded from Catholic communion.

Catalogue of Doctrinal Judgments of the Former Bishops of the Apostolic See on the Grace of God and the Free Choice of the Will (c. 435-442)

The next magisterial text comes from a fifth-century collection of teachings from the Apostolic See that were gathered together by St. Prosper of Aquitaine not long after the reign of Pope Celestine I (422-432), somewhere between 435 and 442.[88] This collection of teachings is referred to as *Doctrinal Judgments of the Former Bishops of the Apostolic See on the Grace of God and the Free Choice of the Will*.[89] The bishop quoted concerning the nature of baptism is Pope Innocent I. The Catalogue states,

> In the transgression of Adam, all men lost their natural capacity and their innocence, and no one can rise from the depths of that collapse through free will unless the

grace of the merciful God lifts him up, as Pope Innocent of blessed memory proclaims and says in his letter to the Synod of Carthage:

> For long ago that man, a victim of his free will in making quite rash use of his goods, fell into the depths of transgression and sank and found no means by which he might be able to rise from there; and, deceived forever by his own freedom, he would have lain under the crushing weight of this collapse if the subsequent coming of Christ had not lifted him up again by virtue of the grace of him who, through *the purification of the new rebirth, has washed away every past fault in his baptismal bath.*[90]

Like everything we've seen so far in Jesus' teaching, Paul's teaching, Peter's teaching, and the early Church Fathers, here it is expressed again through baptism, regeneration takes place, and sins are washed. That's nothing other than salvation.

Second Council of Orange (529)

Next up in our survey is the Second Council of Orange. The council's focus was to refute what is known as *semi-Pelagianism*, the view that humans can, by their own will, *without* grace, choose to enter a relationship with God. The council also affirmed the concept of baptismal regeneration, and not in some vague or loose way, where baptism and regeneration are merely related. Rather, it affirms that baptism is causal. Canon 5 states the following:

> If anyone says that the increase as well as the beginning of faith and the very desire of faith—by which we believe in him who justifies the sinner and by which *we come to the regeneration of holy baptism*—proceeds from our

> own nature and not from a gift of grace, namely, from an inspiration of the Holy Spirit changing our will from unbelief to belief and from godlessness to piety, such a one reveals himself in contradiction with the apostolic doctrine, since Paul says: "I am sure that he who began a good work in you will bring it to completion at the day of Jesus Christ" (Phil. 1:6); and again: "It has been granted to you that for the sake of Christ you should not only believe in him but also suffer for his sake" (v. 29); and also: "By grace you *have been saved through faith*; and this is not your own doing, it is the gift of God" (Eph. 2:8). For those who say that the faith by which we believe in God is natural declare that all those who are strangers to the Church of Christ are, in some way, believers.[91]

There isn't much on baptism itself. However, the flow of the canon indicates that baptism is that which saves. It explicitly speaks of coming to "the regeneration of holy baptism." This statement implies that regeneration happens in and through baptism.

But notice that the canon also speaks of those things that lead up to baptism, and their requirement of grace, in the same breath as those very same things leading to "salvation." This becomes clear when the canon quotes Ephesians 2:8: "By grace you have been *saved* through faith." For the council fathers, the regeneration that occurs in baptism *is* our salvation.

Third Council of Valence (855)

The next stop in our survey of magisterial texts is the Third Council of Valence. In Canon 5 of its *On Predestination*, the council connects baptism with several themes that we've already seen in the teachings of Jesus and Paul: Jesus' regeneration and Paul's baptismal death. Canon 5 states,

> We believe that we must hold most firmly that all the multitude of the faithful—*who have been regenerated* "from water and the Holy Spirit" (John 3:5) and, by this, truly incorporated into the Church and, according to the apostolic doctrine, *baptized into the death of Christ* (Rom. 6:3)—have been *absolved from their sins in his blood*; for there could not have been *true regeneration* in these unless there had also been a *true redemption*; since in the sacraments of the Church there is nothing vain, nothing deceptive, but all is absolutely true and supported by its own truth and sincerity.[92]

Again, the council brings together both themes of regeneration and baptismal death, both of which involves absolution from sins. And each are effects that are brought about through the sacrament of baptism.

Pope Clement V and the Council of Vienne

Let's now fast-forward a bit to Pope Clement V (1305-1314) and the Council of Vienne (1311-1312). In its constitution entitled *Fidei Catholicae* ("The Catholic Faith"), the council condemned a series of errors of one named Peter John Olivi, some of which concerned the theology of baptism. Here's a quote from the constitution confirming the regenerative nature of baptism:

> All are faithfully to profess that there is one baptism that regenerates all those baptized in Christ, just as there is one God and one faith [cf. Eph. 4:5]. We believe that when baptism is administered in water in the name of the Father and of the Son and of the Holy Spirit, it is a perfect means of salvation for both adults and children.[93]

According to the council, it's necessary that Christians confess that baptism saves, for both adults and children. For adults, such salvation would include original *and* personal sin. Concerning children, however, the salvation spoken of here would entail the remission only of original sin, given that children prior to the age of reason can't commit personal sin.

The council goes on to affirm that in baptism, children receive habitual grace (also known as *sanctifying grace*). It states,

> Yet because, as regards the effect of baptism in children, it is found that certain theologians have held contrary opinions, some saying that by baptism *guilt is indeed remitted* in infants but grace is not conferred, others on the contrary asserting that both *guilt is remitted and the virtues and sanctifying grace are infused with regard to habit* though for the time being not with regard to use: We, considering the general efficacy of Christ's death, which through baptism is applied in like manner to all the baptized, choose, with the approval of the sacred council, the second opinion, which says that *sanctifying grace and the virtues are conferred in baptism on both infants and adults*, as more probable and more in harmony with the words of the saints and of modern doctors of theology.[94]

So the Council of Vienne teaches not only that baptism saves by remitting sins, both original and personal, but also that it imparts habitual or sanctifying grace. Such effects are nothing less than the gift of salvation.

Pope Eugene IV and the Council of Florence

Our next stop in this magisterial survey is the "Decree for the Armenians," which is included in Pope Eugene IV's 1439 bull *Exsultate Deo* (Rejoice to God), and was adopted as a decree issued by the Council of Florence. The decree contrasts the "sacraments" of the Old Law and those of the New, and in such contrast the nature of baptism is revealed. The decree states,

> In the fifth place, in order to facilitate the instruction of the Armenians of today and in the future, we reduce the truth about the sacraments of the Church to the following very brief formula. There are seven sacraments of the New Law: namely, baptism, confirmation, Eucharist, penance, extreme unction, orders, and matrimony, which differ greatly from the sacraments of the Old Law. The latter, in fact, did not cause grace, but they only prefigured the grace to be given through the Passion of Christ.
>
> These sacraments of ours, however, both *contain grace and communicate it* to those who worthily receive them. Of these, the first five are ordered to the spiritual perfection of each person in himself, and the last two [are directed] to the governance and the increase of the whole Church. *Through baptism, in fact, we are reborn spiritually.* . . .
>
> Among these sacraments, there are three, namely, baptism, confirmation, and orders, that *imprint an indelible character* on the soul, which is a type of spiritual sign that is distinct from the rest. As a consequence, they may not be repeated in the same person.[95]

Like in prior magisterial statements, baptism is professed to spiritually regenerate, alluding to Jesus' teaching in John 3:3-5. But the decree also affirms that baptism imprints an "indelible character" on the soul, marking us for Christ. So baptism makes us *saved children of God.*

The Council of Trent (1545-1563)

We now come to the Council of Trent. There are three places where the council focuses on baptism. The first is the "Decree on Original Sin," which was promulgated during session five of the council (June 17, 1546). The council infallibly declares:

> If any one denies, that, by *the grace of our Lord Jesus Christ, which is conferred in baptism*, the guilt of *original sin is remitted*; or even asserts that all that which has the true and proper nature of sin is not taken away, but says that it is only erased, or not imputed,—*let him be anathema.*
>
> For, in those who are *born again*, God hates nothing, because there is *no condemnation* to those who are truly buried together with Christ by baptism into death; who walk not according to the flesh, but, putting off the old man, and putting on the new one, who is created according to God, are *made innocent, immaculate, pure, harmless, and beloved of God, heirs indeed of God*, but joint heirs with Christ; so that there is nothing whatever to retard them from *entrance into heaven.*[96]

Here, the Council of Trent brings together everything that went before it. It affirms that baptism communicates grace. But, specifically, it communicates the grace that regenerates us and remits original sin, making us interiorly righteous—"made innocent, immaculate, pure, harmless, and beloved of God." Such interior righteousness makes us fit for entrance into heaven.

The next place where the Council speaks of baptism is Session VI in its *Decree on Justification*. The decree affirms that *justification*—the transference from the state of unrighteousness (i.e., original sin) to the state of righteousness—is brought about *through* baptism. It states,

> By which words a description of *the justification of the impious* is interwoven, to the effect that it is a translation from that state in which man is born a child of the first Adam, into the state of grace, and of the adoption of the sons of God, through the second Adam, Jesus Christ, our Savior. And this translation, since the gospel has been promulgated, cannot be effected, *without the laver of*

> *regeneration*, or the desire thereof, as it is written; Unless a man be born again of water and of the Holy Ghost, he cannot enter into the kingdom of God.[97]

The phrase "laver of regeneration" refers to the sacrament of baptism. And notice that the council, like the whole theological tradition preceding it, within the Church Fathers and within magisterial teaching, roots the belief that baptism justifies us in Jesus' Born Again discourse (John 3:3–5).

The council further confirms baptism as the cause of our salvation in chapter seven of the aforementioned decree. But the focus is precisely on which *type* of cause baptism is, and teaches that it is the *instrumental* cause of salvation. Here's the relevant text:

> Of this justification the causes are these: The final [cause] indeed is the glory of God and of Christ, and eternal life; while the efficient cause is the merciful God, who gratuitously washes and sanctifies, sealing, and anointing with the Holy Spirit of promise, who is the earnest of our inheritance; but the meritorious cause is his most beloved only-begotten, our Lord Jesus Christ, who, when we were enemies, for the great charity wherewith he loved us, merited justification for us by his most holy passion on the wood of the cross, and for us made satisfaction unto God the Father; *the instrumental cause, moreover, is the sacrament of baptism*, which is the sacrament of faith, *without which justification never befell any man.*[98]

Notice that at the end of the above quote, the council affirms, again, that baptism causes justification. But, as it specifies, the nature of its causal activity is that of an instrument. In other words, God *uses* the sacrament of baptism as an instrument *through* which *he* communicates saving grace.

The *instrumental causality* of baptism is important because some Christians might be inclined to think that if we say baptism saves, then we're implying that Jesus *doesn't* save. But as is clear from the above passage, nothing could be further from the truth. The council affirms that Jesus merited for us the grace of salvation. He is the *ultimate*, or *primary* cause of our salvation. To say that baptism saves means simply that God wills baptism to be the means through which he applies or communicates the saving grace that Christ merited for us.

The council's seventh session sums up its teaching on the salvific efficacy of baptism in canon five of its Canons on the sacrament of baptism. The canon states, "If anyone shall say that baptism is free—that is, not *necessary unto salvation*—let him be anathema."[99]

The Catechism of the Catholic Church

Our last stop in this magisterial survey is the *Catechism of the Catholic Church*. The *Catechism* articulates the Church's belief about baptism in several places throughout. Thus, rather than quoting passages in full, this section will weave together into a coherent whole the various parts.

The *Catechism* defines baptism as the sacrament in which believers are "reborn as sons of God" (1213) by "water and Spirit" (John 3:5). It incorporates us into the mystical body of Christ (1 Cor. 12:13) and makes us sharers in the mission of the Church. "Just as the gestation of our first birth took place in water, so the water of baptism truly signifies that our birth into the divine life is given to us in the Holy Spirit" (CCC 694). This divine life in the Spirit, also known as sanctifying grace (2023), is the reason why St. Peter can say in 2 Peter 1:4 that in Christ we become "partakers of the divine nature."

"New birth in the Holy Spirit" (1262) is not the only principal effect of baptism that the *Catechism* identifies. There is another: "purification from sins." The *Catechism* states, "By baptism *all sins* are forgiven, original sin and all personal sins" (1263). And it's not just sins that are forgiven in baptism; "all punishment for sin" is remitted as well. The purification that takes place in baptism is so complete that in those who are "reborn nothing remains that would impede their entry into the kingdom of God, neither Adam's sin, nor personal sin, nor the consequences of sin, the gravest of which is separation from God."

These two principal effects of baptism—new birth in the Spirit and purification from sins—are, according to the *Catechism*, brought about within the soul by the gift of sanctifying grace, also called "the grace of justification" (1266), that the Holy Spirit infuses in baptism (2024). "Sanctifying grace is the the gratuitous gift of his life that God makes to us . . . to heal it of sin and to sanctify it" (2023), thus making us "pleasing to God" (2024). In the words of Paul, sanctifying grace is that which makes us "a new creation" (2 Cor. 5:17).

Now, this doesn't mean that baptism takes away all temporal consequences of sin, such as suffering, illness, death, and frailties inherent in life, like weakness of character and the inclination to sin (called *concupiscence*). In God's wisdom, we're left to "wrestle with" these consequences knowing that "an athlete is not crowned unless he competes according to the rules" (CCC 1264; cf. 2 Tim. 2:5).

In addition to grace, baptism also imparts what the Church throughout the centuries has called a sacramental "seal" (CCC 1121; cf. chapter twelve of this book). It's a spiritual "mark" on the soul that identifies us as belonging to the Lord, and it enables us to "share in Christ's priesthood" and be "a member of the Church according to different states and function."

If we remain faithful to what this seal demands of us—being a faithful witness to Christ—then we will depart this life "marked with the sign of faith" and receive the inheritance of eternal life that is ours by virtue of this seal. As Paul writes, we are "heirs of God and fellow heirs with Christ" (Rom. 8:17). St. Irenaeus's label for baptism is thus apt: "the seal of eternal life."[100]

Baptism also gives the soul supernal powers that enables it to live and act on a supernatural level. These powers come with the gift of sanctifying grace. One set of powers is called the *theological virtues*: faith, hope, and love. Faith enables the Christian to believe in God and everything revealed by God (CCC 1814). Hope enables the believer to trust in God's promises (1817). Love, or charity, enables the believer to love God above all things and our neighbor out of love for God (1822).

Another set of powers is called the gifts of the Holy Spirit, which enable the believer to "live and act under the prompting of the Holy Spirit." (1266). There are seven in number: wisdom, knowledge, understanding, counsel, fortitude, piety, and fear of the Lord (1831; cf. Isa. 11:2).

There are various names for the sacrament, each of which is rooted in some aspect of its nature. For example, it is called *baptism* after to the ritual of immersing the person, or washing a part of the person (the top of the head), in water. The Greek word for "baptize," *baptizein,* means to "plunge" or "immerse." The immersion under water signifies "burial into Christ's death, from which we rise up by resurrection with him (CCC 1214; cf. Rom. 6:3-4).

The sacrament is also called "the washing of regeneration and renewal by the Holy Spirit." It is so named because of the new birth of water and Spirit that the sacrament actually brings about, the birth without which no one "can enter the kingdom of God" (John 3:5).

Another name for the sacrament is *enlightenment*. The *Catechism* explains the reason for this name as follows:

> This bath is called *enlightenment*, because those who receive this [catechetical] instruction are enlightened in their understanding." . . . Having received in baptism the Word, "the true light that enlightens every man," the person baptized has been "enlightened"; he becomes a "son of light," indeed, he becomes "light" himself (1216).

The *newness* that baptism brings for the believer makes it "the gateway to life in the Spirit" (CCC 1213). It gives the soul a new *life*. It gives the soul a new state—a *sanctified* state. It gives the soul new *powers*. It gives the soul a new identity as a child of God. No wonder the Church has identified baptism as "the basis of the whole Christian life." The whole of the Christian's supernatural life, therefore, has its roots in the sacrament of baptism (1266).

Conclusion

As our above survey shows, the belief that baptism saves runs throughout the centuries of magisterial teaching. And this teaching is nothing new. It coheres perfectly with what we saw in our survey of both early Christian testimony among the Church Fathers and the New Testament evidence as found in Jesus' teaching, Paul's teaching, and Peter's teaching. The evidential case for the belief that baptism saves is, therefore, robust and solid. To deny such a belief is to deny part of the historic Christian faith.

With the evidence now in place, we can turn to questions that pertain to the *practice* of baptism. This will be the focus of our next section—chapters six through nine.

Part II

The Practice

Chapter 6

The Minister and the Recipient

When it comes to the practice of baptism, questions arise as to who can administer it and who can receive it. At first glance, such questions might seem a bit pedantic, something only for theological nerds. But as we'll see, these questions are at the heart of many of the conversations that we Catholics have about baptism, whether we're talking to Catholics or Protestants. So let's start with questions that pertain to the appropriate *minister* of the sacrament.

Who Can Baptize?

The Non-Ordained?

According to the *Catechism*, the "ordinary ministers of baptism are the bishop and priest and, in the Latin Church, also the deacon." However, in the case of necessity, "*anyone*, even a non-baptized person," can baptize (1256, emphasis added). "Necessity" here *commonly* is understood as a situation where there is danger of death or a situation where no ordinary minster is available for a prolonged period.

The three necessary conditions for validity must be met. First, the proper matter must be used: water. Second, the person who baptizes must do so with "the required intention." This entails that the person "will to do what the Church does when she baptizes." Knowledge of the nature of baptism or what it does is not required. Third, "the trinitarian baptismal formula" must be used (1216)—'I baptize you in the name of the Father, and of the Son, and the Holy Spirit.'"

The teaching that anyone can baptize was definitively taught in 1215 by the Fourth Lateran Council. The council's confession of faith reads,

> The sacrament of baptism (which is celebrated in water at the invocation of God and the undivided Trinity, that is, the Father, the Son, and the Holy Spirit) conduces to the salvation of children as well as of adults when duly conferred by anyone according to the Church's form.[101]

Pope Eugene IV reaffirmed this teaching in his 1439 papal bull *Exsultate Deo.* He added to Lateran IV's declaration by highlighting the need for proper intention:

> The minister of this sacrament is the priest, to whom by reason of his office it belongs to baptize. But in case of necessity not only priests or deacons, but also laymen or laywomen or even pagans and heretics may baptize, provided they observe the Church's form and *intend to do what the Church does.*[102]

We can look to St. Thomas Aquinas for the rationale behind this teaching.[103] Aquinas starts with the idea that "in those things which are necessary for salvation, man can easily find the remedy."[104] He roots this in the mercy of God, which is expressed in God's desire to save all men (1 Tim. 2:4). Reasonable enough.

Aquinas then, in agreement with Catholic teaching (CCC 1257), identifies baptism as "the most necessary among all the sacraments."[105] This leads him to conclude, and rightly so, that "lest man should have to go without so necessary a remedy, it was ordained, both that the matter of baptism should be something common that is easily obtainable by all, i.e. water;

and that the minister of baptism should be anyone, even not in orders, lest from lack of being baptized, man should suffer loss of his salvation."[106]

The *Catechism* concurs with Aquinas's reasoning: "The Church finds the reason for this possibility in the universal saving will of God and the necessity of baptism for salvation" (1256).

The practice of allowing others besides the ordinary ministers of baptism—bishop, priest, or deacon—to administer the sacrament dates to around the turn of the third century. Initially, permission was restricted to *baptized* laity, and particularly lay *men*. Tertullian, writing in the second century, admitted that in the case of necessity a baptized layman could administer baptism. In his work *On Baptism*, he writes,

> Beside these [bishops, priests, and deacons], even laymen have the right; for what is equally received can be equally given. Unless bishops, or priests, or deacons, be on the spot, other disciples are called to the work. The word of the Lord ought not to be hidden by any: in like manner, too, baptism, which is equally God's property, can be administered by all.[107]

For Tertullian, "laymen" referred strictly to a *male* layperson. He didn't think women were able to baptize.[108] This belief that laymen could baptize in emergency situations was confirmed later by the fourth-century Synod of Elvira,[109] St. Jerome,[110] and St. Augustine.[111] The first mention of the permissibility of women administering baptism is found in the Middle Ages.[112]

It wasn't until the eighth century, at the Synod at Compiègne (757),[113] that the Church permitted *unbaptized* persons to administer baptism. Pope Nicholas I, more than a century later (866), confirmed the Synod of Compiègne's teaching.[114]

Heretics?

This was a divisive issue in the third century. Great bishops, the likes of St. Cyprian of Carthage, taught that heretics *could not* validly administer baptism.[115] At the time, Pope St. Stephen I appealed to Tradition and authoritatively opposed Cyprian on this issue.[116]

Others, like St. Augustine, would follow suit and teach that heretics *could* validly administer baptism. Augustine famously defended this view in his work *On Baptism, Against the Donatists*.

The Council of Trent settled the issue in the sixteenth century, infallibly teaching that a heretic can validly administer baptism: "If any one shall say, that the baptism which is also given by heretics in the name of the Father, and of the Son, and of the Holy Ghost, with the intention of doing what the Church doth, is not true baptism; let him be anathema.[117]

Grandparents in Secret?

Given the above teaching that *anyone* can baptize, grandparents often find themselves wondering if they are permitted to baptize their grandchild when his parents don't want him baptized. And not just grandparents, but also caring individuals. I've had folks ask me this question countless times. It demands a thorough response.

Let's start with what we *shouldn't* do: baptize the child in secret. The *Code of Canon Law* (CIC) states that "for an infant to be baptized licitly . . . the parents or at least one of them or the person who *legitimately* takes their place must consent" (868 §1-1). And this would be true not just for infants, but also for any child under the age of reason, along with anyone who "habitually lacks the use of reason" (for example, someone with a mental illness or developmental disability) (97 §2; 99).

There are a few things to note here. First, consent by a parent or someone who takes his place is necessary for the baptism to be *licit*. But even an illicit baptism in this case would still be *valid*—that's to say the child would be reborn and receive the graces of the sacrament, but it would be done in a way that contravenes Church law. In other words, if someone knows about this law, it would be immoral to contravene it, and he would sin in doing so.

The second thing to note is the canon's point about someone "legitimately" taking the place of the parent. This is directed explicitly at the idea that someone might try to baptize a child in secret without the parents' (or a parent's) express permission.

Another condition for licit baptism is that there must be a reasonable hope that the child will be raised Catholic. Sections 1-2 of canon 868 in the CIC state the following:

> There must be a founded hope that the infant will be brought up in the Catholic religion; if such hope is altogether lacking, the baptism is to be delayed according to the prescripts of particular law after the parents have been advised about the reason.

The canon does, however, go on to specify that the above prescript is void in the danger of death:

> An infant of Catholic parents or even of non-Catholic parents is baptized licitly in danger of death even against the will of the parents (§2).

Now, naturally, the question becomes "Why?" Why does the Church forbid baptisms of children under the age of reason against the will of the parents? There are several reasons.

First, it is contrary to natural justice. Determination of what a child under the age of reason does and receives is naturally *due* to the parents. Thomas Aquinas teaches as much:

> Those who do not yet have the use of free will (a child under the age of reason), according to the natural law . . . are under the care of their parents as long as they cannot look after themselves.[118]

To baptize a child under the age of reason against the will of his parents, therefore, would be to deprive the parents of what is naturally due to them. And to deprive parents of what is naturally due to them is an injustice. Such an act would be just as much a violation of natural justice as it would be to attempt to baptize a person having the use of reason against his will. (As we'll see below, it wouldn't work, but it's still an injustice to try.)

Aquinas gives another reason behind the Church's prohibition of baptizing children against the will of their parents: It makes the child liable to unbelief. He writes,

> Moreover under the circumstances it would be dangerous to baptize the children of unbelievers; for they would be liable to lapse into unbelief, by reason of their natural affection for their parents. Therefore it is not the custom of the Church to baptize the children of unbelievers against their parents' will.[119]

One last reason that we'll give here is that to baptize against the parents' will is to thwart an aspect of the *directionality*, or goal-directedness, of the gift of faith.[120] The *Catechism* teaches that baptism is a "sacrament of faith," and the faith that is given in baptism is "called to develop" and "needs the community of believers" (1253).

To baptize a child knowing that the gift of faith imparted to him will not be nourished and developed by a community of believers would be to thwart the very natural directionality of the gift itself, kind of like when people thwart the directionality of the sexual act in the use of contraception, or the directionality of the act of eating by intentionally vomiting the food, or the directionality of the communicative act of assertion by lying.

Now, I sympathize with the person who says, "But this is urgent and serious. Wouldn't you rescue a child from the danger of physical death? Why wouldn't you do the same in the case of spiritual death?"

Aquinas also deals with this sort of objection and provides an insightful answer.[121] He starts with a principle that I think most would agree upon—namely, we can't go and rescue someone from physical death *against the order of civil law*. For example, if a judge condemns a man to death on account of a proportionate crime, we wouldn't be morally permitted to use force to rescue the man from death. The reason is that such a judgment is issued by legitimate authority, and it's immoral for us to act against such authority.

Similarly, as Aquinas teaches, we shouldn't try to rescue a child from spiritual death against the will of the parents lest we infringe on the order of the natural law. The order of the natural law dictates that parents have the natural right to determine the actions of their children under the age of reason. And to baptize a child against his parents' will would violate such an order.

But someone might still counter, "Don't we belong more to God than to man? It's God who gave us our soul, the *primary* principle within us. Only our bodies, which are lower in the hierarchy of being, have been given to us by our parents. Thus, it would seem it's not unjust for a child to be baptized against his parents' will."

Again, here we appeal to the natural order articulated above: The actions of a child under the age of reason are subject to being determined by the parents. Here's how Aquinas answers this sort of objection:

> Man is ordained unto God through his reason, by which he can know God. Wherefore a child, before it has the use of reason, is ordained to God, by a natural order, *through the reason of its parents*, under whose care it naturally lies, and it is according to their ordering that things pertaining to God are to be done in respect of the child.[122]

The bottom line is that although we belong to God more than to man, it's God who willed the natural order. Therefore, to act against this natural order by baptizing a child under the age of reason against his parents' will would be to act against God himself. And that's something we ought always to avoid.

Now that we know what we *shouldn't* do when our loved ones don't plan on baptizing their children, let's talk about what we *can* do or say.

One easy thing is to extend an invitation. Sometimes all it takes is a simple invitation for the parents to baptize their child. Given the distractions that our society has to offer young parents, and the lack of faith formation that is often present in people's lives growing up, some parents simply may have never even considered baptism for their child. (Of course, it is important to be prudent here: if a baptism will awaken a long-dormant faith in the parents, it absolutely should be done, but this might not be the best course for faithless parents who might use it as an excuse for a party and then forget about it.)

You can also share with the parents the Church's teaching on baptism and its spiritual effects. This would be not merely to convince them that it's a good thing to baptize their child; also, we want to help lead the parents to conversion, creating within them a desire for regeneration and union with Christ.

Start by asking if they'd be interested in knowing why the Church thinks baptism is so important. If they express that they're open to talking about it, then you can share with them the various spiritual gifts that baptism gives, the most important being salvation. And if you struggle to find the right words, then you can always just give them this book and pray that the Spirit will move their hearts.

Okay, now that we've addressed the question of *who* can baptize, let's move to the question of *who can receive* baptism.

Who Can Receive Baptism?

The Non-Baptized?

The *Catechism* states it plainly: "Every person not yet baptized and only such a person is able to be baptized" (1246). The "not yet" part is rooted in the Church's teaching that a valid baptism can be received only once. This teaching came to the fore during the early centuries, when the Church dealt with the issue of whether heretics who repented had to be rebaptized. St. Cyprian of Carthage, a third-century bishop, was a leading figure who advocated for the rebaptism of heretics.[123] Pope St. Stephen I[124] opposed Cyprian on this issue, and later popes[125] and councils[126] would reaffirm and uphold Stephen's teaching.

Adults and Infants?

Regarding the age at which a person can receive baptism, the answer is all ages. Both adults *and* infants are cable of receiving baptism. Concerning adults, the *Catechism* states, "Since the beginning of the Church, adult baptism is the common practice where the proclamation of the gospel is still new" (1247). For such individuals, preparation for baptism, also known as "the catechumenate," plays an important role. It is meant to "dispose the catechumen [the person preparing to receive baptism] to receive the gift of God in baptism, confirmation, and the Eucharist."

The legitimacy of the practice of infant baptism would be affirmed over and over throughout the centuries and finally defined infallibly at the Council of Trent:

> If any one shall say, that infants, for that they have not actual faith, are not, after having received baptism, to be reckoned amongst the faithful, and that, for this reason, they are to be rebaptized, when they have arrived at years of discretion; or, that it is better that the baptism of such be omitted, than that they, while not believing by their own act, should be baptized in the faith alone of the Church; let him be anathema.[127]

Unlike in the case of adults, the practice of infant baptism is not explicitly attested to in Scripture. This is reasonable, given that much of the New Testament chronicles the conversion of adults. However, there are biblical foundations that support infant baptism along with historical testimony. Given that infant baptism lies at the heart of most conversations about baptism, it deserves an entire chapter of its own. Therefore, we're going to save our treatment of the biblical and historical foundations of infant baptism for our next chapter.

Infants in the Womb?

Speaking of infants, what about an infant in the womb? Could we baptize an infant in the womb if he is in the danger of being miscarried? The short answer is "no," since there is no practical way to apply the matter of water. Remember, the *matter* of water is one of the three conditions (the other two being *form* and *intention*) necessary for a valid baptism. The reason for this is that baptism is a physical act of washing that bestows supernatural grace. A person can't baptize by mere intention alone. That means that the minister of baptism must be able to sprinkle or pour water on the baby, or immerse the baby in water, which cannot be done when the baby is surrounded in the womb with amniotic fluid.

Now, there's also a *theological* rationale for why baptism can't be administered to an infant in the womb. St. Thomas Aquinas argues along these lines, rooting the rationale in St. Augustine. Aquinas writes,

> On the contrary, Augustine says (Ep. ad Dardan.): "No one can be born a second time unless he be born first." But baptism is a spiritual regeneration. Therefore no one should be baptized before he is born from the womb.[128]

The idea here is that since baptism is revealed by our Lord to be a *second* birth (John 3:3-5), albeit a *spiritual* birth, it shouldn't be given until one has *already* been born a first time with his physical birth (whether naturally or through a C-section). To baptize prior to the first birth would be an act at odds with the nature of baptism itself.

The Unintentional?

The above two categories of individuals—namely, infants within and outside the womb—have to do with individuals who, at their particular stage of development, don't possess the ability to actively intend baptism. So this raises a question: "What about someone who *is* at a stage of human development where such an active intention is within their power? Would their active intention to receive baptism be required for a valid baptism?" The answer is yes.

If you've ever been to a baptism, you know that part of the ritual is for the priest to ask the adult seeking baptism, called a *catechumen*, "What do you ask of the Church?" And the catechumen can answer, as one option, "Baptism." (Other options include "faith" and "entry into the Church.") Notice that there must be an expressed intention to receive the sacrament on the part of the catechumen.

There is also a theological rationale to this.[129] Consider that baptism involves death to the old life of sin and the beginning of a new life in Christ. Well, death to the old life of sin requires repentance, which in turn necessarily presupposes the will's active intention to repent. So too, the beginning of a new life in Christ, which is given through baptism, necessarily presupposes the will's active intention to receive baptism.

The Persistent Sinner?

But what if someone has an active intention to receive baptism and yet still chooses to persist in or cling to a sin? Can such a person be baptized? The answer depends on what we mean by "can."

If by "can" we mean, "Will the person be *validly* baptized?", then the answer is yes. Aquinas teaches that such a baptism would be valid insofar as it communicates the "seal" or "indelible mark" mentioned in previous chapters (cf. CCC 1121)—that's to say, the individual would be regenerated and marked as a child of God the Father.

However, the *effects* of the seal, such as the communication of sanctifying grace and the remission of sins (and everything involved with sin, such as temporal punishment due to sin), would not be produced in the soul. And only once the person repents of the persistent sin (ordinarily through the sacrament of reconciliation), which at the time serves as an obstacle to the effects of the baptismal seal being produced, would such effects in fact be produced.

Now, if by "can" we mean, "*Should* someone be baptized if he persists in a sin?", then the answer is no. There are three reasons.[130]

First, baptism incorporates us into Christ. Paul says, "For as many of you as were baptized into Christ have put on Christ" (Gal. 3:27). For a person to persist in sin is to set his will against being united to Christ, given that union with Christ and sin are mutually exclusive ("What partnership have righteousness and iniquity?"—2 Cor. 6:14).

Secondly, baptism in this scenario would become a performative contradiction, an act where the agent performing the action intends something contrary to what the act is naturally about. For example, if I say, "I am dead," the very utterance of the sentence falsifies the meaning of the words. Or if someone engages in the sexual act, which naturally is ordered to the generation of children, and yet actively thwarts the achievement of such a goal or end, then he falsifies the meaning of the act itself. Given the irrationality built into these actions, reason recognizes that we ought to avoid them.

Similarly, the will to persist in sin while voluntarily getting baptized thwarts baptism from achieving one of the ends or goals to which it is ordered: the remission of sin. As Aquinas puts it, "no one having the will to sin can, at the same time, be cleansed from sin . . . for this would be to combine two contradictory things."[131] One ought not to engage in such perverse behavior, especially when it comes to sacrosanct things like the sacrament of baptism.

Thirdly, we shouldn't lie. The very act of someone presenting himself to the waters of baptism visibly signifies that he is voluntarily seeking the cleansing and remission of sins. Yet, insofar as he wills to persist in sin, he is *not* seeking the cleansing and remission of sins, since the two are mutually exclusive. Now, as Aquinas puts it, "a sign is false if it does not correspond with the thing signified."[132] Since in this scenario the sign of a man presenting himself for baptism doesn't correspond, or map on to, what it signifies—namely, repentance of sin—we have a bearing of false witness, which is something that we ought not do.

Adults Who Can't Use Reason?

Another category of people that is often asked about is adults who, for whatever reason, are severely mentally impaired such that they can't use their rational faculties of intellect and will, whether such an adult was under this condition from birth or acquired it later.

Concerning those who would be in such a state from birth, the same line of reasoning that the Church employs for justifying the baptism of children under the age of reason would apply. So these people could receive the sacrament.

But for those who once had intellectual lucidity and only became impaired later—say, through a brain injury—it would depend on what their wishes were when they had full use of their faculties. If, for example, a person had expressed a desire to be baptized before becoming rationally impaired, then baptism should be administered to him. If, on the other hand, prior to the mental impairment, a person never expressed a desire to be baptized, then baptism should not be administered.

What about if a person's mental impairment isn't permanent, and at times he has moments of lucidity? Well, if he were to express a desire to be baptized during such a time, then it would be appropriate to baptize him, even if he were to fall back into mental impairment. However, if a person were not to express any desire for the sacrament during this time of lucidity, then the sacrament ought not to be administered, just like how we wouldn't attempt to baptize any adult without his express intention to be baptized.

The Dead?

There's one last group that we must ask about: the dead. This question about the dead arises due to a statement that Paul makes in 1 Corinthians 15:29: "What do people mean by being baptized on behalf of the dead? If the dead are not raised at all, why are people baptized on their behalf?"

It's generally agreed that whatever baptism this was, it was not administered *to* the dead—that's to say, baptizing the corpse.

But even if Paul were describing Christians engaging in this ritual, there's no indication that he approves it. In fact, the Synods of Hippo (393) and Carthage (397) condemned such baptisms.[133]

Others have interpreted this "baptism" as a representative ("vicarious") baptism, in which a person was baptized *on behalf of* someone who had died to obtain the baptismal graces for that deceased person.[134] Still others have interpreted it as a baptismal ceremony that the person being baptized viewed as a way to intercede for his deceased loved ones.[135]

Regardless, Paul's point is that such baptisms are futile without belief in a future resurrection.[136]

Conclusion

The type of questions covered in this chapter show clearly that this is not some academic exercise for the theologian in the ivory tower. It doesn't get any "closer to home," so to speak, than wondering whether you can secretly baptize your grandson because his parents won't, or whether you can baptize a dying child in the womb, or whether you can baptize your child who has severe mental impairments, or whether you can baptize your loved one who has died. This testifies to the fact that theology integrates itself throughout, or touches, all the nooks and crannies of human life.

Speaking of "nooks and crannies of human life" and being "close to home," our children are about as close as it gets. Above we said that the Church teaches that we must baptize infants. But some Protestants reject this teaching. Why do they reject it? What evidence do we have for it? To these questions we turn in our next chapter.

Chapter 7

Infants Too or Only Adults?

In our previous chapter, we talked about recipients who can properly receive the sacrament of baptism. And we mentioned briefly that infants fall within that category. Such a belief is held by most Christians—e.g., Catholic, Orthodox, Anglicans, Lutherans, Methodists, Presbyterians, and United Protestants.

However, there are some who reject infant baptism, such as Baptists, Anabaptists, Pentecostals, Assemblies of God, and Church of Christ. Given that this is a hot-button issue for such groups, it's important that we give it due treatment.

The current chapter is divided into basic sections: 1) arguments in favor of infant baptism and 2) arguments against it. I will address each in turn.

Arguments in Favor

At the outset we must confess that the New Testament neither explicitly *instructs* Christians to baptize infants nor gives *examples* of the practice. However, a biblical case can be made on account of certain things revealed to us in Scripture.

From Jesus' Call for Infants to Be Brought to Him

Consider, for example, Jesus' explicit command for his disciples to allow children to approach him. Luke records it this way:

> Now they were bringing even infants to him that he might touch them; and when the disciples saw it, they rebuked them. But Jesus called them to him, saying, "Let the children come to me, and do not hinder them; for to such belongs the kingdom of God. Truly, I say to you, whoever does not receive the kingdom of God like a child shall not enter it" (Luke 18:15-17).

The first thing to note is that the children brought to Jesus were "infants." The Greek word here is *brephos*, which primarily means "a child that is still unborn, fetus," and secondarily means "a very small child, baby, infant."[137]

Secondly, Jesus says the kingdom of God is for such infants.[138] Well, the kingdom is also for adults. So, if adults are proper recipients of baptism on account of the kingdom belonging to them, then it's reasonable to conclude that infants would also be proper recipients of baptism on account of Jesus saying the kingdom belongs to them as well.

From Colossians 2:11-12

A second biblical argument comes from Paul's teaching in Colossians 2:11-12 that baptism is the New Testament fulfillment of circumcision. He writes,

> You were circumcised with a circumcision made without hands, by putting off the body of flesh in the circumcision of Christ; and you were buried with him in baptism, in which you were also raised with him through faith in the working of God, who raised him from the dead.

It's important to note here that the Greek word for *and* (*kai*) is not present in the original text. It literally reads, "You were circumcised with . . . the circumcision of Christ, *having been* buried with him in baptism."[139] This means that baptism *is* the "circumcision of Christ." Martin Luther acknowledged as much: "We now have baptism instead of circumcision."[140]

According to Genesis 17:10–12, every male child was to be circumcised at eight days old. Children were made members of God's covenant not by the use of their reason, but based on the faith of their parents.

Given that baptism is the new circumcision—the gateway into the New Covenant—to say that children under the age of reason can't be baptized is to say that children under the age of reason could be incorporated into the Old Covenant but not the New Covenant. That would make the New Covenant less inclusive than the Old, which doesn't fit with the general theme of inclusivity that marks the New Covenant (see Matt. 28:19–20, Gal. 3:8). The New Covenant is open to every nation and people on earth—but not to little children? That's absurd!

Some Protestants would still answer "no," baptism is *not* for little children. And the reason is because they're not convinced by the argumentation from Colossians 2:11–12. Our good ol' friend Todd Baker offers a couple of comebacks that challenge the parallel between baptism and circumcision.

One comeback is that circumcision was a rite that of its nature was restricted to signifying incorporation into the *nation of Israel* and *physical descent* from Abraham. By contrast, so Baker argues, "entrance into the New Covenant is not gained by a rite, ceremony, or religious act, but is for all people—men, women, and children—who voluntarily profess their belief in the Lord Jesus Christ."[141] Baker doesn't elaborate beyond these words how the New Covenant being for all people proves that baptism is not the new circumcision, so we're left to speculate. But the implication seems to be that if we say baptism is the new circumcision, then we're thereby limiting the scope of New Covenant membership because circumcision was limited.

The problem with Baker's counterargument is its assumption: *If we draw a parallel to something in the Old Testament, then the parallels must be exact.* But this is simply false. We don't say Jesus must be sinful to say he is the new Adam. We don't say Jesus' sacrifice must be offered within the Temple to be the new and definitive atoning sacrifice. We don't say Gentiles must be excluded from the Christian community because Christians are the new "Israel of God" (Gal. 6:16).

Moreover, Jesus sets a precedent for expanding on things that were restrictive in the Old Testament. For example, he broadens the scope of the act of adultery beyond the physical act to include the interior act of the will ("everyone who looks at a woman lustfully has already committed adultery with her in his heart"—Matt. 5:27). He reveals that it's not what goes into a person's body that defiles him, but what comes from the heart (Mark 7:19-22). And it's well known that Isaiah's prophecy in 7:14 ("Behold, a virgin shall conceive and bear a son, and shall call his name Immanuel") on the literal historical level was a reference to the young maiden Abijah and her son King Hezekiah. Granted, no one believes that Hezekiah's birth was a *virgin* birth, but the Hebrew word used in Isaiah 7:14, *almah*, can be translated as either "virgin" or "young maiden." (The Greek word *parthenos* does primarily mean "virgin.") Given this, we can see how Matthew, inspired by the Spirit, can interpret the text in a broader way, extending it to include Mary, a virgin, conceiving Jesus by supernatural means (Matt. 1:23).

So if Jesus and the New Testament authors could expand upon and broaden the scope of things in the Old Testament that point toward and are fulfilled by things in the New, then surely we can interpret Paul's teaching on baptism as the new circumcision as not being restrictive, like the old circumcision, but being more expansive to include "all people—men, women, and children," to quote Baker.

Baker offers another comeback. He writes,

> One looks in vain in the Old Testament to find a passage that flatly says circumcision saves. . . . The Scripture constantly affirms the act of circumcision did not save anyone or grant spiritual regeneration.[142]

Baker's argument seems to be that if we're going to say baptism is the circumcision of the New Covenant, and thereby argue for infant baptism, then the Old Testament would have to have spoken of the salvific efficacy of circumcision. Since it doesn't, Baker reasons, baptism can't be the circumcision of the New Covenant. And if that's the case, then we can't appeal to such a parallel to support infant baptism.

The first problem with Baker's counterargument is that he fails to realize that a New Testament fulfillment is meant to be *greater* than the type.[143] Circumcision in the Old Covenant was meant to be merely a *type* of baptism. Thus, we'd expect the fulfillment of circumcision—baptism—to be more glorious than its type. And the fulfillment *is* more glorious, insofar as it saves, whereas the type did not.

Now, there is a sense in which circumcision *did* play *some* role in the individual being justified in the sight of God. Insofar as people obeyed God's command to circumcise every male, they remained within God's covenantal family and thereby were just in the sight of God. But whereas circumcision was merely a sign, the new circumcision—baptism—communicates that which it signifies—namely, salvation. And here the New Testament fulfillment shines more glorious than the type.

From the Universal Nature of Jesus' Born Again Discourse

Jesus' Born Again discourse in John 3:5 implies that children would need the second birth. Recall that Jesus says, "Unless one is born of water and the Spirit, he cannot enter the kingdom of God." The Greek word that's translated "one" is *tis*, which means "anyone." [144] The word has an *indefinite* or non-restrictive sense, thereby implying *any* human being.[145] Jesus didn't say unless an *adult* is born again.

Now, does a child fall within the category of "anyone"? Yes! Therefore, baptism is for *all* human beings, young and old, because Jesus "wills that *all* be saved and come to the knowledge of the truth" (1 Tim. 2:4).

From the Reality of Original Sin

Our next argument for infant baptism is rooted in the Christian claim that infants are conceived with "original sin," what the Council of Trent called "the death of the soul."[146] The *Catechism* reaffirmed this definition (403) and added a key nuance: original sin is called sin "only in an analogical sense: it is a sin 'contracted' and not 'committed'—a state and not an act" (404).[147] Our argument from original sin can be laid out in the following syllogistic form:

> Premise One: Those who need spiritual birth—i.e., salvation—need the sacrament of baptism.
>
> Premise Two: Infants need spiritual birth—i.e., salvation.
>
> Conclusion: Therefore, infants need the sacrament of baptism.

Premise one is supported by the arguments we've given in previous chapters for the salvific efficacy of baptism. Baptism *regenerates* us (John 3:5), it *buries* us with Christ and *raises* us to a new life in him (Rom. 6:3–4), it puts us *in* Christ (1 Cor. 12:13), and it saves us (1 Peter 3:21). Given that the sacrament of baptism gives the gift of salvation, it follows that anyone who needs such a gift should receive it through baptism.

But do infants need this gift? Premise two in our argument says yes. Let's see if we can make good on this claim.

The biblical text that the Magisterium has appealed to as evidence for this belief is Romans 5:12: "Therefore as sin came into the world through one man and death through sin, and so death spread to all men because all men sinned." The Council of Trent appeals to this verse in its Decree Concerning Original Sin. The *Catechism* appeals to it, too, along with Romans 5:18-19, in its teaching that original sin is a consequence of Adam's sin for all of humanity (402).

But where does the Magisterium get off interpreting Romans 5:12 as a reference to original sin?

We can start by making a simple either-or statement: Paul has to be talking about either personal sin or original sin. (Personal sin means the sins we commit ourselves, whether they're venial or mortal.) Now, if we can show that it's not personal sin, then it would follow that he's talking about original sin.

How might we establish that Paul is not talking about personal sin?

Well, consider this question: Which members of the human race can't possibly be guilty of personal sin? Clearly, one answer is infants. Another is the severely mentally handicapped. So if we can show that infants and the severely mentally handicapped must be numbered among the "all" who sinned, then it will follow that Paul is thinking of original sin.

The key for proving that infants and the severely mentally handicapped must be numbered among the "all" is the connection that Paul makes between death and sin: "death spread to all men because all men sinned." Notice that Paul draws a parallel between the "all" that constitutes the group who "have sinned" and the "all" that constitutes the group to whom "death spread." Moreover, Paul sees the death that extends to all as an effect of the sin that extends to all.

Do infants and the severely mentally handicapped die? Yes. Given the parallel between the two groups, it follows that infants and the mentally handicapped are included within the category of "all have sinned." And if that's the case, then Paul is not thinking of personal sin here; he's thinking of original sin.

Now, someone might counter, "If we say that whoever dies is included within the category of 'all have sinned,' then we must say that Jesus and Mary would have to be included there because they both died (or at least Jesus, if we want to say Mary didn't die). But to say that Jesus and Mary are included in the 'all have sinned' category is absurd."

In response, this would be true if and only if we didn't have a source of knowledge other than Jesus' and Mary's humanity for knowing that they were exceptions to the rule.

For example, we can say it belongs to the nature of a human being as a corporeal being—a being with a mortal body—to die. So when I, knowing this, observe that Aristotle has died, I can reasonably infer that Aristotle is a corporeal being.

But suppose that it's revealed that God will preserve Aristotle (or, we might argue, Elijah or Enoch) from death. Given that he doesn't die, must I conclude that he's not a corporeal being? Of course not. I know that he still belongs to the category of corporeal beings, even though he doesn't die, because I have something other than Aristotle's nature for determining whether he will die: God's revelation.

Similarly, although death belongs to those who have contracted the sin of Adam by nature, it doesn't follow that Jesus and Mary must have contracted the sin of Adam by nature because they died. The reason is that we have something other than Jesus' and Mary's death and human nature for determining whether they have contracted Adam's sin: God's revelation.

But we don't have any such revelation when it comes to infants and the severely mentally handicapped. This being the case, the death that they experience is seen as evidence for being included among the group "all have sinned," because Paul clearly teaches that death extends to all as an effect of the type of sin that he's speaking of.

Given that infants and the severely mentally handicapped are included in Paul's category of "all have sinned," and we know that such members of the human race in principle cannot commit personal sin, it follows that in Romans 5:12, Paul is thinking about original sin and not personal sin.

There's another line of argumentation that we can use here. Consider that the "all have sinned" refers to either a) every human being, including those humans who can't sin personally, like infants and the severely mentally handicapped, or b) only human beings who have committed personal sin.

Now, if Paul is referring only to humans who have committed personal sin, then such people would be included within the category of "all have sinned" by imitation of Adam. But if that's the case, then death would extend only to those who commit personal sin, since Paul clearly teaches that death extends to all who are included within the category "all have sinned": "death spread to all men because all men sinned." Surely, death doesn't extend only to those who commit personal sin. Infants and the severely mentally handicapped also die.

Therefore, the "all have sinned" cannot refer only to human beings who have committed personal sin. Rather, it must refer to every human being, including those humans who can't personally sin. And it follows that personal sin is not Paul's target here in Romans 5:12. Rather, his target is original sin.

Original sin is not just something that we infer from the craziness of sin that we see on our nightly cable news channels.

It's part and parcel of God's revelation. *All* humans, including infants, come into existence with such a condition of the soul. Therefore, *all* humans, including infants, need spiritual birth, which just is salvation. Given that premises one and two in our argument are true, the conclusion must necessarily be true: infants need the sacrament of baptism.

From Early Christian Testimony

A question that might arise at this juncture is whether our belief in and practice of infant baptism is attested to by early Christian sources. The answer is *yes*. The historical evidence dates back as early as the second and third centuries.

One witness to the practice is St. Irenaeus of Lyon. In his *Against Heresies* (A.D. 189), he affirms that infants can be born again:

> He came to save all through means of himself—all, I say, who through him are born again to God—*infants*, and children, and boys, and youths, and old men.[148]

We know that Irenaeus has baptism in mind here because elsewhere in his writings, he identifies this second birth with baptism:

> And [Naaman] dipped himself . . . seven times in the Jordan [2 Kings 5:14]. It was not for nothing that Naaman, when suffering from leprosy, was *purified upon being baptized, but as an indication to us*. For as we are lepers in sin, we are made clean of our old transgressions *by means of the sacred water and the invocation of the Lord; we are spiritually regenerated as newborn babes*, even as the Lord has declared: "Except a man be born again through water and the Spirit, he shall not enter into the kingdom of heaven" [John 3:5].[149]

Another witness is Hippolytus. Recall that he was a third-century prolific theologian. In his *Apostolic Tradition* (215), he writes,

> First *baptize the little ones*; if they can speak for themselves, they shall do so; if not, their parents or other relatives shall speak for them.[150]

What about the great early to mid-third-century scriptural exegete Origen? He writes (c. 246),

> The Church has received the tradition from the apostles to give baptism even to little children. For they to whom the secrets of the divine mysteries were committed were aware that in everyone was [original] sin's innate defilement, which needed to be washed away through water and the Spirit.[151]

Origen argues along the same lines when he writes elsewhere, "Since the baptism of the Church is given for the forgiveness of sins, that, according to the observance of the Church, that baptism also be given *to infants*."[152] His rationale for this practice is that there *is* something "in infants that ought to pertain to forgiveness and indulgence"; otherwise, "the grace of baptism would appear superfluous," which, for Origen, it can't be.[153]

Another witness to infant baptism in the early Church is St. Cyprian of Carthage. During his time, the early to mid-200s, Cyprian was dealing with a controversy over whether Christians should model the Jewish practice of circumcision and hold off baptism until the eighth day after birth. Here is how Cyprian responds in one of his letters:

> In respect of the case of the infants, which you say ought not to be baptized within the second or third day after

> their birth, and that the law of ancient circumcision should be regarded, so that you think that one who is just born should not be baptized and sanctified within the eighth day, we all thought very differently in our council. For in this course which you thought was to be taken, no one agreed; but we all rather judge that the mercy and grace of God is not to be refused to anyone born of man.[154]

The above passages, from Irenaeus to Cyprian, suffice to show that infant baptism is, in the words of the *Catechism*, an "immemorial Tradition of the Church" (1252) to which we should hold fast.

Arguments Against

To the above conclusion—that we should hold fast to the "immemorial Tradition of the Church"—some Christians would counter, "Not so fast! Maybe this is a tradition. But it's not a tradition that we *should* hold fast to."

Why would a Christian reject such a tradition? Well, there are several reasons. Let's look at some of them here.

The Baby Cannot Exercise Faith

One main argument against infant baptism is that an infant is unable to have faith. Christians who make this argument root it in what Jesus says: "He *who believes* and is baptized will be saved" (Mark 16:16).[155] Christians who oppose infant baptism see this as clear evidence that baptism is to be given only to those who have professed faith in Christ. This is why it's sometimes called a "believer's baptism."

If belief must precede baptism, it's argued, and infants can't profess belief, since they can't reason yet, it follows that infants can't be baptized. To baptize them would go against the instruction of Jesus.

There are three ways that we can respond.

First, Jesus doesn't say that belief precedes baptism. He simply makes belief a condition for salvation *along with* baptism. Nowhere in Scripture does Jesus say, "He who believes *first*, and *then* is baptized, will be saved." Belief *and* baptism are two conditions for salvation, without any stipulation as to the order.

For an adult, of course, faith will come first, because faith is what leads him to the waters of baptism (CCC 1262). But for an infant who is baptized, the faith of the parents and of the Church suffices. As Aquinas teaches in his *Summa Theologiae*, the faith of the parents, and indeed the whole Church, "profits the child through the operation of the Holy Ghost," because the child, before the use of reason, "believes not by himself but by others."[156] This being the case, the child receives salvation "not by [his] own act, but by the act of the Church."

This doesn't mean that the infant won't have to personally make an act of faith in Christ as he comes to the age of reason. Such a profession will be necessary on condition that the child comes to know the truth of God's revelation. But for an infant, the faith of the parents and the Church suffices, thus meeting both of Jesus' conditions for salvation: belief and baptism.

Second, the idea that the faith of the parents and the Church suffices to meet the faith condition is consistent with Jesus' practice of administering blessings on behalf of the faith of others.

Consider, first, the passage that we looked at before—Luke 18:15-17, where Jesus instructs his disciples to let the "infants" be brought to him and says the kingdom of God belongs to them. Jesus is not opposed to children being members of his kingdom even though they can't make an act of faith. Thus, giving our children over to the Lord in baptism, even though they can't make an act of faith, is consistent with Jesus' desire for children to be brought to him.

Furthermore, there are examples in the Bible where Jesus administers blessings specifically on behalf of the faith of the parents. Take Jesus' decision to raise Jairus's daughter from the dead (Mark 5:22-23, 35-43). The young girl makes no profession of faith in Christ, yet Jesus still performs the miracle. And we can infer that it was on behalf of Jairus's faith, because Jesus tells Jairus, "Do not fear, only believe" (v. 36). That Jesus then performed the miracle tells us that Jairus *did* believe.

Similarly, in Mark 9:14-27, Jesus exorcizes a demon-possessed boy in response to his father's request, even though the boy has no faith. Mark makes explicit that Jesus performs the exorcism in response to the *father's* faith: "Jesus said to him . . . 'All things are possible to him who believes.' Immediately the father of the child cried out and said, 'I believe; help my unbelief!'" (vv. 23-24). If a parent's faith sufficed for Jesus to physically raise a girl from the dead and free a boy from demonic possession, then it's reasonable to conclude that a parent's faith can suffice for a child under the age of reason to receive the blessings of baptism.

We can also consider the household baptisms mentioned in Scripture. For example, when the Philippian jailer asks Paul what he must do to be saved (Acts 16:30), Paul responds, "Believe in the Lord Jesus, and you will be saved, you *and your household*" (v. 31). We're then told that Paul spoke the "word of the Lord" to the jailer and his household that evening, after which they were all baptized (vv. 32-33). Notice that the jailer's faith was sufficient to bring the blessing of baptism upon his entire family, members of which may have been children under the age of reason.

Other examples of household baptisms administered on behalf of the faith of the parent are Lydia's household (Acts

16:15) and the household of Stephanas (1 Cor. 1:16). It's true that we don't know for sure that these households had children under the age of reason. Nevertheless, blessings still come upon these households on behalf of the faith of the parents.

Finally, even deniers of infant baptism make an exception for infants when it comes to the general rule of the necessity to have faith *to be saved*.[157] Whenever the New Testament authors speak of the necessity to believe in Christ to be saved, they never say "except for infants." Rather, they simply assert, "Faith in Christ is necessary for salvation."

Yet Protestants must allow infants to be an exception, lest they instantaneously condemn all infants to hell. If a Protestant is willing to allow infants to be an exception to the general rule that one must believe in Christ *to be saved*, then he can hardly criticize Christians for seeing infants as an exception to the general rule that one must believe in Christ *to be baptized*.

From the Concern that Infant Baptism Downplays the Role of Faith

Now, a Protestant might concede for argument's sake that an infant can be an exception to the general rule of the necessity to believe in Christ to be baptized. But then he might argue that infant baptism causes people to downplay the role of faith. Here's how Gavin Ortlund puts the argument in his dialogue with apologist Trent Horn:

> That's why I think that my pastoral concern comes up is, people think that baptism saves. When an infant is brought to the font and water in the name of the Trinity is put on the infant, they just passed into a state of regeneration. I don't believe that, but it's an invitation to see it through my eyes. If you don't think it's in that, can you see how this is going to cause people to downplay the

> role of faith? Not that it needs do that, but that it often does, it seems to me.[158]

The first thing to say in response is that the abuse of something doesn't negate its rightful use. Just because some people might lose sight of the role of faith in practicing infant baptism, that doesn't mean the problem is with infant baptism itself. The problem most likely is with the person not being properly catechized to know the importance of *his* faith in baptizing the child.

As mentioned above, the "faith" condition for baptism is met by the faith of the parents (or guardian) who bring the child to receive the sacrament. That faith is necessary, is evidenced by the questions posed to the parents during the ceremony:

> Celebrant: You have asked to have your child baptized. In doing so you are accepting the responsibility of training him (her) in the practice of the faith. It will be your duty to bring him (her) up to keep God's commandments as Christ taught us, by loving God and our neighbor. Do you clearly understand what you are undertaking?
>
> Parents: We do.
>
> Celebrant: Dear parents and godparents: You have come here to present this child for baptism. By water and the Holy Spirit he (she) is to receive the gift of new life from God, who is love. On your part, you must make it your constant care to bring him (her) up in the practice of the faith. See that the divine life which God gives him (her) is kept safe from the poison of sin, to grow always stronger in his (her) heart. If your faith makes you ready to accept this responsibility, renew now the vows of your own baptism. Reject sin; profess your faith in Christ

> Jesus. This is the faith of the Church. This is the faith in which this child is about to be baptized.

The celebrant then goes on to ask a series of questions that pertain to whether the parents and godparents reject Satan and his works, along with whether they belief the articles of faith professed in the Creed. Given this emphasis on the necessity for the parents to exercise faith in Christ, if someone loses sight of the importance of faith, it's not the practice of infant baptism itself that's the culprit. Rather, it's the individuals bringing the child for baptism, or the pastors who fail to offer them proper catechesis.

From the New Testament Examples of Only Adults Being Baptized

Some Protestants might object to infant baptism on account of the instances where baptism is administered in the New Testament, each of which involves not infants, but only adults (e.g., Acts 2:41; 8:12, 38; 10:48; 16:15, 33; 1 Cor. 1:14-16).[159] It would seem that infant baptism wasn't practiced by the first-century Christians. And if that's case, then neither should we.

One problem with this objection is that it makes a false inference. The conclusion—"the earliest Christians didn't practice infant baptism"—doesn't follow from the premise "all the examples in the New Testament involve only adults."

One reason is that we don't know for sure that all instances of baptism in the New Testament involved *only* adults, as the argument claims. For example, when Luke tells us that the entire households of Lydia (Acts 16:15) and the jailer (Acts 16:33) were baptized, there *could* have been children, and even children under the age of reason.

Not mentioning children, even when it's reasonable to assume that there were children, would be consistent with what we find elsewhere in the New Testament. For example, when recounting the miracle of the multiplication of the loves and fishes, Mark (6:44), Luke (9:14), and John (6:10) simply tell us there were "five thousand *men*." They don't include the children. Yet Matthew tells us that children were there (14:21), though even he, interestingly, excludes the children, along with the women, from the number five thousand.

So the idea that children—even those under the age of reason—were present in the households who were baptized, despite not being mentioned, is quite plausible.

Similarly, when Paul tells us that he baptized the household of Stephanas (1 Cor. 1:16), we don't know for sure that it involved *only* adults. There very well could have been infants who were part of Stephanas's household.

Conclusion

The arguments for infant baptism are quite strong. We have teachings from Paul that at least provide biblical grounds for the *allowance* of infants to be baptized. We have Jesus' teaching in the Born Again discourse that would seem to *demand* we baptize infants. And we have explicit evidence from extra-biblical Christian sources in the first and second centuries of Christians professing the *validity* of infant baptism.

But the arguments in favor become even stronger when we see that the arguments *against* infant baptism fail. In the end, we leave our fellow Christian brethren who reject infant baptism with the words of the Lord: "Let the children come to me, and *do not hinder them*; for to such belongs the kingdom of God" (Luke 16:18).

Chapter 8

Immersion or Pouring?

The *Catechism* teaches that baptism is validly conferred "by pouring the water three times over the candidate's head" (1239). But is this mode valid?

Some Christians who practice baptism, like the Church of Christ and Baptists, say "no," it's not valid. The only valid baptism is by way of *immersion*. But why do they say this?

Below, we're going to consider some arguments that Christians give to justify the immersion-only view. And then we'll look at some arguments against it. Unlike in the previous chapter, where we argued in favor of the proposition and defended it against challenges, here we're doing the opposite: we're arguing *against* the proposed view and critiquing its defense.

So let's get started with the reasons why some Christians believe in baptism by immersion only.

Arguments in Favor of Immersion-Only

From Immersion Examples in the New Testament

Some Christians appeal to actual baptisms that occur in the New Testament and argue that since those people were fully immersed, immersion must be the only valid mode.[160] For example, Mark tells us that when Jesus was baptized, he "came up out of the water" (Mark 1:10). Luke records that the Ethiopian eunuch "went down into the water" when he was baptized by Philip (Acts 8:38).

One response is that the narratives concerning Jesus' baptism and the baptism of the Ethiopian eunuch don't specify that immersion was the mode of baptism used. Let's take Jesus' baptism first. All Mark tells us is that Jesus "came up out of the water." Of course, it *could* mean that he was immersed. But it could also mean that he simply came out of the water in the sense that he came up onto the shore of the Jordan River. He might have waded into the river up to his waist and had water poured on his head. The text itself is silent as to the mode of baptism.

With regard to the eunuch in Acts 8:38, we have a bit more detail that sheds light on what Luke meant. Notice that Luke says that "*they both* went down into the water." Then, afterward, "*they* came up out of the water." This suggests that Luke is not using that expression to convey baptism by immersion. He is simply telling us that the eunuch and Philip went down into the water together, and they both came out together—not that they were both immersed. Philip, having been baptized already, would not have immersed himself as he baptized the eunuch!

Additionally, even if these events did involve immersion baptisms, it doesn't follow that immersion is the only valid mode of baptism. The only thing it would prove is that some Christians *practiced* immersion baptisms. It wouldn't imply anything about whether they believed that it was the *only* valid mode.

For example, some Catholic churches practice full immersion baptisms. But that doesn't mean they believe that immersion baptism is the *only* valid mode.

From the Greek Word Baptizō

Now, a Christian who rejects non-immersion baptisms might concede that mere instances of immersion baptism don't prove it's the only valid way. However, he won't give up his thesis, because he believes he can root it in something more robust—namely, the very meaning of the Greek word *baptizō,* which means "to immerse."[161]

The problem with this argument is that although *baptizō* means "to immerse," sometimes it's used in other ways. For example, in Scripture, it's associated with *pouring out* relative to the Jewish ritual washings, and it thus gives grounds for denying the claim that *baptizō* means only immersion baptism.

Consider, for example, a passage from Mark's Gospel that refers to Jewish ceremonial washings. In the third chapter, Mark records that the Pharisees and scribes were appalled at how Jesus' disciples "ate with their hands defiled, that is, unwashed" (v. 1). Mark then gives a commentary on the "baptismal" washings that Jesus' apostles failed to uphold:

> For the Pharisees, and all the Jews, do not eat unless they wash their hands, observing the tradition of the elders; and when they come from the market place, they do not eat unless they purify [Greek, *baptisōntai*] themselves; and there are many other traditions which they observe, the washing [Greek, *baptismous*] of cups and pots and vessels of bronze (vv. 3–4).

According to the *Jewish Encyclopedia*, the baptismal washing of hands may be performed either by pouring *or* immersion:

> The pouring on of water was a sign of discipleship. Thus, Scripture says of Elisha that he poured water (2 Kings 3:11) upon the hands of Elijah, meaning that he was his disciple. The hands may also be purified by immersion; but in that case the same rules must be observed as in the case of immersion of the entire body in a regular ritual bath, or *miḳweh.*[162]

Since Mark describes the Jewish ritual washing of hands with the word *baptizō*, and such Jewish ritual washings could be performed either by pouring or immersion, we have biblical grounds for associating *baptizō* with the pouring.

We also have biblical grounds from the outpouring of the Holy Spirit on the Day of Pentecost.[163] Peter sees in the event of Pentecost the fulfillment of Joel's prophecy, which says the Holy Spirit will be "poured out" upon God's people: "I will pour out my Spirit upon all flesh" (Joel 2:28; cf. Acts 2:16–17).

Now, prior to this event, Jesus specifically calls this outpouring the "baptism of the Holy Spirit." Recall what he told the disciples: "You heard from me, for John baptized with water, but before many days you shall be *baptized* [Gk., *baptisthēsesthe*] with the Holy Spirit." (Acts 1:4).

So, "baptism," at least the one in the Holy Spirit, is associated with the imagery of "pouring." If the "baptism of the Holy Spirit" is not restricted to immersion but also associated with pouring, then water "baptism" doesn't have to be restricted to immersion, but can also be associated with pouring. From this it follows that it's unbiblical to restrict the word *baptizō* to immersion baptisms.

Arguments Against Immersion-Only

From the Doctrine of Sola Scriptura

Matthew 28:19 is the text where Jesus commissions the disciples to go out and make disciples by baptizing them. He even gives the specific formula: "Baptize them in the name of the Father, and of the Son, and of the Holy Spirit."

But notice that Jesus specifies *only* the formula. He doesn't specify *the way* baptism is to be administered. So an "immersion-only" Christian can't appeal to this passage to justify his belief. Nor can he reasonably appeal to any other passage in the Bible, as we've shown above. This being the case, the lack of biblical evidence for the instruction to baptize by immersion only creates a problem for the Protestant who believes that only baptisms by immersion are valid.

Given the Protestant's belief in *sola scriptura*—that Scripture alone is his infallible rule of Christian faith and practice—he would have no grounds to demand that Christians be baptized *only* by immersion. To say that only baptisms by immersion are valid is to believe something that's not accounted for by the sole infallible rule of faith—the Bible. Therefore, any Protestant who believes that only baptisms by immersion are valid is violating *sola scriptura*.

From Ezekiel 36:24-25

Another argument against immersion-only baptisms comes from Ezekiel 36:24-25, which we already looked at in a previous chapter. Recall, in reference to the time of the Messiah, God says through the prophet Ezekiel,

> I will take you from the nations, and gather you from all the countries, and bring you into your own land. I will *sprinkle clean water upon you*, and you shall be clean from all your uncleannesses, and from all your idols I will cleanse you. A new heart I will give you, and a new spirit I will put within you; and I will take out of your flesh the heart of stone and give you a heart of flesh. And I will put my spirit within you, and cause you to walk in my statutes and be careful to observe my ordinances.

As mentioned before, the *Jewish Encyclopedia* says of this time:

> To receive the spirit of God, or to be permitted to stand in the presence of God (his *Shekinah*), man must undergo baptism . . . in the messianic time God will himself pour

> water of purification upon Israel in accordance with Ezekiel 36:25.[164]

Since Ezekiel's prophecy refers to baptism in the messianic age, and it describes this messianic baptism as God "sprinkling" water upon his people, we have good biblical grounds to think baptism can be validly administered in ways other than full immersion.

From Practical Issues in Acts 2:38

The idea that immersion is the only valid way to baptize runs into a bit of an obstacle when we consider the baptisms that took place on the Day of Pentecost in Acts 2. Recall that Luke tells us that 3,000 people converted that day, and Peter told them they needed to be baptized. Assuming they were baptized that day, it's extremely implausible that they would have all been immersed. As the Catholic Answers tract puts it: "Archaeologists have demonstrated there was no sufficient water supply for so many to have been immersed."[165] And the Jordan river wouldn't have been an option, given that it was a forty-minute car ride from Jerusalem.

Even if there had been enough water, it's unlikely that the natives of Jerusalem would have allowed their city's water supply to be polluted by three thousand unwashed bodies being immersed in it.[166] It's more reasonable to conclude that the three thousand folks who converted that day were baptized either by pouring or by sprinkling.

From General Practical Issues

More practical issues abound for immersion-only baptism. There are *general* practical difficulties that make it nearly or entirely impossible for some people to undergo immersion baptism, like people with medical conditions—the bedridden, quadriplegics, those who have recently undergone a surgical procedure, etc. Certain environments would also make immersion baptism difficult for some people, such as nomads in the desert or inhabitants of frigid climates. If immersion were the only valid form of baptism, at certain places and times, it would be a practical impossibility.

From Early Christian Testimony

A major obstacle to the immersion-only baptism view is that it's *not* part of the historic Christian faith. We have evidence from early Christian testimony that they believed the opposite: non-immersion baptisms *are* valid.

The earliest record is the *Didache*, also known as *The Teaching of the Twelve Apostles*, which is an early Christian handbook dating to around A.D. 50 to 70. It gives the following instructions on how to baptize:

> And concerning baptism, thus baptize ye: Having first said all these things, baptize into the name of the Father, and of the Son, and of the Holy Spirit, in living water. But if thou have not living water, baptize into other water; and if thou canst not in cold, in warm. But if thou have not either, *pour out water thrice upon the head* into the name of Father and Son and Holy Spirit.[167]

The first few modes of baptism mentioned here could refer to immersion (though they don't have to). But the explicit mention of *pouring* that follows makes it clear that even in the mid-first century, pouring was considered a valid form.

The next early witness we have is St. Hippolytus (215). In his *Apostolic Tradition*, he gives instructions concerning baptism. He seems to presume that the sacrament will be administered by way of immersion. But he allows for non-immersion baptisms when the need arises. He writes,

> At cockcrow prayer shall be made over the water. The stream shall flow through the baptismal tank or pour into it from above when there is no scarcity of water; but if there is a scarcity, whether constant or sudden, then use whatever water you can find.[168]

Hippolytus knows no such thing as non-immersion baptisms being invalid.

Pope Cornelius (251) also testifies to the validity of non-immersion baptisms in his Letter to Fabius of Antioch. In speaking of Novatian after he received his exorcism, Cornelius writes, "As he seemed about to die, he received baptism by *affusion* [pouring], on the bed where he lay."[169]

St. Cyprian of Carthage provides another historical example of the validity of the pouring method of baptism. In his Letter to a Certain Magnus (Letter 75), which dates to around 255, Cyprian addresses the specific question of whether pouring is a valid form of baptism:

> You have asked also, dearest son, what I thought of those who obtain God's grace in sickness and weakness, whether they are to be accounted legitimate Christians, for that they are not to be washed, but sprinkled, with the saving water. . . . In the sacraments of salvation, when necessity compels, and God bestows his mercy, the divine methods confer the whole benefit on believers; nor ought it to trouble anyone that sick people seem to be sprinkled or affused, when they obtain the Lord's grace.[170]

Conclusion

Whenever the arguments in favor of your belief fall short, and you have both the Bible and early Christian testimony opposing it, you're not in a good position to demand that Christians adopt your belief. Well, that's exactly the case for the immersion-only baptism view. Its arguments fail to prove that only immersion baptisms are valid, and it has both biblical and historical evidence weighing against it.

Sure, immersion baptism expresses the reality of baptism most profoundly. But for the reasons given above, no Christian should ever feel pressured to believe that their baptism was *invalid* because he wasn't immersed, but only had water poured over him.

With the question of the mode (or way) of baptism now settled, we must ask, "What's the proper formula?" Is it the trinitarian formula: "In the Name of the Father, and of the Son, and of the Holy Spirit"? Or is the proper form "In the name of Jesus"? To this question we turn in our next chapter.

Chapter 9

The Trinitarian Formula or "In the Name of Jesus"?

When it comes to the formula to use for baptism, the Catholic Church prescribes the trinitarian formula: "In the name of the Father, and of the Son, and of the Holy Spirit." Pope Eugene IV taught as much in his 1439 bull *Exsultate Deo*, also known as the Council of Florence's Decree for the Armenians. It states:

> Among all the sacraments, holy baptism holds the first place because it is the gateway to the spiritual life.... The matter of this sacrament is true natural water; it does not matter whether it is cold or warm. The form is: "I baptize you *in the name of the Father and of the Son and of the Holy Spirit.*"[171]

The validity of the trinitarian formula was infallibly reaffirmed by the Council of Trent in canon four of its canons on baptism in the Decree on the Sacraments, stating,

> If anyone shall say, that the baptism which is also given by heretics in the name of the Father, and of the Son, and of the Holy Ghost, with the intention of doing what the Church doth, is not true baptism; let him be anathema.[172]

The *Catechism* echoes this teaching in paragraph 1240. It states,

> In the Latin Church this triple infusion is accompanied by the minister's words: "N., *I baptize you in the name of the Father, and of the Son, and of the Holy Spirit.*" In the Eastern liturgies the catechumen turns toward the East and the priest says: "The servant of God, N., is baptized *in the name of the Father, and of the Son, and of the Holy Spirit.*" At the invocation of each person of the Most Holy Trinity, the priest immerses the candidate in the water and raises him up again (emphasis added).

The question now becomes whether there is biblical and historical evidence for this formula. And this becomes relevant in conversations because some Christians reject the trinitarian formula as valid, advocating the "in the name of Jesus" formula in its place.

Thus, below we're going to give arguments in support of the trinitarian formula and then assess whether the arguments for the "in the name of Jesus" formula succeed.

Arguments in Favor

From Matthew 28:19

Our first argument for the trinitarian formula comes from Matthew 28:19. Before his ascension into heaven, Jesus gives the explicit command as to *how* the apostles were to baptize the nations: "Go therefore and make disciples of all nations, baptizing them *in the name of the Father and of the Son and of the Holy Spirit.*" Regardless of what Christians think about the "in the name of Jesus" formula, a Christian *at least* can't reject the trinitarian formula as valid since it comes from the lips of the Master himself.

From Acts 19:1-5

Our first argument proved that the trinitarian formula at least must be valid. This argument from Acts 19:1-5 strongly suggests that the early Christians *in fact* used the trinitarian formula.

Luke tells us that Paul passed through the upper country of Ephesus and found some believers there (v. 1). Paul asked them, "Did you receive the Holy Spirit when you believed?" (v. 2). The believers responded, "No, we have never even heard that there is a Holy Spirit." Puzzled as to why they had never heard of the Holy Spirit, Paul asked, "Into what then were you baptized?" (v. 3). They responded, "Into John's baptism" (v. 4).

The implication here is that these believers in Ephesus *should* have heard of the Holy Spirit if they had been baptized with the right baptism—Jesus' baptism. If the formula were in Jesus' name only, then Paul's question would make no sense. The question itself, therefore, implies that the Holy Spirit was expected to be used in the ritual when believers were baptized, like in the trinitarian formula that Christ commands the apostles to use in Matthew 28:19.

From Early Christian Testimony

For our third argument, we move to early Christian testimony outside the boundaries of the Bible. The earliest record outside the Bible for the use of the trinitarian formula is the *Didache*, which is an early Christian handbook dating to around A.D. 50 to 70. It gives the following instructions on how to baptize:

> Concerning baptism, thus baptize ye: having first said all these things, baptize into *the name of the Father, and of the Son, and of the Holy Spirit*, in living water. But if thou have not living water, baptize into other water; and

> if thou canst not in cold, in warm. But if thou have not either, *pour out water thrice upon the head into the name of Father and Son and Holy Spirit.*[173]

Next up for our historical survey is Justin Martyr. We've already looked at the passage where Justin affirms the trinitarian formula in a previous chapter. However, we didn't emphasize the trinitarian formula because our focus was on Justin's belief in the salvific efficacy of baptism. Here is the relevant text, where he affirms the use of the trinitarian formula:

> Then they are brought by us where there is water, and are regenerated in the same manner in which we were ourselves regenerated. For, *in the name of God, the Father and Lord of the universe, and of our Savior Jesus Christ, and of the Holy Spirit*, they then receive the washing with water.[174]

Irenaeus of Lyon also witnesses to the Christian use of the trinitarian formula. In his *Demonstration on the Apostolic Preaching* (c. A.D. 180-190), he writes,

> We have received baptism . . . *in the name of God the Father, and in the name of Jesus Christ*, the Son of God, who was incarnate and died and rose again, *and in the Holy Spirit of God.*[175]

Hippolytus is another witness, although his description of how the trinitarian formula is used differs from other sources. Nevertheless, he believed that the person was baptized in the name of the Trinity. Here's what he writes in his *Apostolic Tradition* (215):

> When he who is being baptized goes down into the water, he who baptizes him, putting his hand on him, shall say thus: *Dost thou believe in God, the Father Almighty*? And

> he who is being baptized shall say: I believe. Then holding his hand placed on his head, he shall baptize him once. And then he shall say: *Dost thou believe in Christ Jesus,* the Son of God? . . . And when he says: I believe, he is baptized again. And again he shall say: *Dost thou believe in [the] Holy Ghost?* . . . He who is being baptized shall say accordingly: I believe, and so he is baptized a third time.[176]

Tertullian also affirms the validity of the trinitarian formula around the same time as Hippolytus. In *Against Praxeas* (216), he writes,

> After his resurrection he promises in a pledge to his disciples that he will send them the promise of his Father; and lastly, he commands them *to baptize into the Father and the Son and the Holy Ghost,* not into a unipersonal God. And indeed it is not once only, but three times, that we are immersed into the Three Persons, at each several mention of their names.[177]

Notice here that Tertullian appeals to Jesus' instruction recorded in Matthew 28:19: "Go therefore and make disciples of all nations, baptizing them *in the name of the Father and of the Son and of the Holy Spirit.*" For Tertullian, Jesus was establishing the form of the sacrament with these words.

Similarly, Origen appeals to Jesus' commission in Matthew 28:19 as proof for the trinitarian formula. And he does so to argue *against* those who baptized only in the name of Christ. Here's what he writes in his Commentary on Romans (248):

> Why, when the Lord himself told his disciples that they should *baptize all peoples in the name of the Father and of the Son and of the Holy Spirit*, does this apostle [Paul] employ the name of Christ alone in baptism, saying, "We who

> have been baptized into Christ"; for indeed, legitimate baptism is had only in the name of the Trinity.[178]

Cyprian of Carthage follows the same line of reasoning as that of Tertullian and Origen. He appeals to Matthew 28:19, writing,

> When, after the resurrection, the apostles are sent by the Lord to the heathens, they are bidden to baptize the Gentiles "*in the name of the Father, and of the Son, and of the Holy Ghost.*" How, then, do some say, that a Gentile baptized without, outside the Church, yea, and in opposition to the Church, so that it be only in the name of Jesus Christ, everywhere, and in whatever manner, can obtain remission of sin, when Christ himself commands the heathen to be baptized in the full and united Trinity?[179]

Our last witness in this historical survey is Eusebius of Caesarea. Like those who preceded him, he appeals to Matthew 28:19 as evidence for the validity of the trinitarian formula in his Letter to the People of His Diocese (323):

> We believe . . . each of these to be and to exist: the Father, truly Father, and the Son, truly Son, and the Holy Ghost, truly Holy Ghost, as also our Lord, sending forth his disciples for the preaching, said, "Go teach all nations, *baptizing them in the name of the Father and of the Son, and of the Holy Ghost.*" Concerning whom we confidently affirm that so we hold, and so we think, and so we have held aforetime, and we maintain this faith unto the death, anathematizing every godless heresy.[180]

Given the evidence from both Scripture and early Christian testimony as to the Christian use of the trinitarian formula, no one can reasonably reject such a formula as a valid form for the sacrament of baptism. To state it differently, a Christian must *at least* affirm the validity of the trinitarian formula.

Arguments Against

Some Christian denominations outside mainstream Protestantism, such as Oneness Pentecostals, argue that the trinitarian formula ("In the Name of the Father, Son, and Holy Spirit") doesn't match with what the Bible has to say about baptism. They claim that baptism should be administered only "in the name of Jesus."

For support, they appeal to passages like Acts 2:38, where Peter says, "Repent, and be baptized every one of you *in the name of Jesus Christ* for the forgiveness of your sins; and you shall receive the gift of the Holy Spirit" (emphasis added).

Other passages include Acts 8:14–15 (with reference to those in Samaria who had received the Word of God), 10:48 (with reference to Cornelius and his Gentile friends), and 19:5 (with reference to believers in Ephesus). Passages like these give rise to a legitimate question: Why is the Church saying that we can baptize with the trinitarian formula when all the baptisms in the Bible are done "in the name of Jesus"?

One response is that Jesus' instruction that includes the trinitarian formula is distinct in nature from the "in the name of Jesus" passages found in the book of Acts. In Matthew 28:19, Jesus is addressing ministers whom he is sending to *perform* baptisms. It stands to reason, therefore, that Jesus would give them the formula to use in administering the sacrament.

This instruction stands in contrast with the "in the name of Jesus" passages found in the book of Acts. Take Peter's injunction in Acts 2, for example, which is in a public setting and is given not to those who would be performing baptisms, but to those who would receive baptism.

Second, Peter's injunction was not premeditated. He is quickly enumerating what must be done to be saved in response to those present who upon hearing his preaching were "cut to the heart" and asked him, "Brethren, what shall we do?" It's unreasonable to think that Peter would be giving precise instructions as to the *words* that must be used in baptism when the occasion calls for him merely to say, "You want to be saved? Okay, here are the things you need to do—repent and get baptized."

Concerning Peter's command for Cornelius to be baptized "in the name of Jesus Christ" in Acts 10:48, like on the Day of Pentecost, Luke records what Peter says to those who will receive baptism, not those who would administer it.

Moreover, Luke is not recording what Peter said specifically. He merely narrates in summary form, "And he [Peter] commanded them to be baptized in the name of Jesus Christ." It doesn't seem that Luke intends to say that the words "in the name of Jesus" were the actual words used in administering baptism.

The other "in the name of Jesus" passages (Acts 8:14-16, 19:5) are even further removed from the nature of Jesus' instructions in Matthew 28:19. They aren't instructions at all.

Each instance is merely a passing reference to the fact that some were baptized: "They had only been baptized in the name of the Lord Jesus" (Acts 8:14-16), and "they were baptized in the name of the Lord Jesus" (Acts 19:5). It's unlikely that such cursory remarks were meant as an articulation of the exact words used for those baptisms.

If "in the name of Jesus" is not the formula, then why all the talk about "in the name of Jesus"? It's likely that the early Church used the "in the name of Jesus" formula to distinguish Jesus' baptism from other types of baptism: Johannine baptism and Jewish ritual washings.

Our above examination of Acts 19:1-5 already gives evidence that Christian baptism wasn't the only baptism in town, since some were administering John the Baptist's baptism of repentance (see also Matt. 3:13-14, 21:25; Acts 1:22, 10:37). Even the Jewish ceremonial washings were considered as a baptism of sorts. For example, in Luke 11:37-38, the Pharisees invite Jesus to dine with them, and Luke tells us that the Pharisees are "astonished to see that he [Jesus] did not first wash before dinner." The Greek word for "wash" is *ebaptizthē*, the root of which is *baptizō*.

Similarly, in Mark 7, we're told that when the Pharisees return from the marketplace, they do not eat unless they first "purify" (Greek, *baptisontai*) themselves (v. 3). Other traditions involve the "washing" (Greek, *baptismous*) of cups and vessels (v. 4). So Jewish ceremonial washings were considered a sort of "baptism."

With John's baptism being so prominent at the time of Christ, and with all the Jewish ritual "baptismal" washings, there would be a need to distinguish Jesus' baptism—"in the name of Jesus"—from all these other kinds of "baptisms." We see this play out in Acts 19, where, after Paul realizes that the believers in Ephesus were baptized only into John's baptism, we're told that "they were baptized in the name of the Lord Jesus" (v. 5), signifying that they were baptized *into* Jesus.

We find something similar in the *Didache*. As mentioned above, it gives the trinitarian formula as the words to use for baptism in chapter seven. And then in chapter nine, it refers back to that same baptism as baptism "in the name of the Lord" (9.5). So for the early Christians, baptism "in the name of the Lord," or "in the name of Jesus," signified *trinitarian* baptism.

We might summarize our above responses in a single thought: The passages that refer to people being baptized "in the name of Jesus" don't undermine the use of the trinitarian formula, since they weren't meant to give instruction as to the words that must be used for baptism. Rather, they were meant only to signify that people were being baptized with Jesus's baptism, as opposed to some other Jewish baptism.

Is the "In the Name of Jesus" Formula Invalid?

Notice that the above argumentation was directed merely at *defending* the trinitarian formula against the claim that the Bible teaches that the "in the name of Jesus" formula is the only valid form for the sacrament. But such a defense doesn't tell us one way or the other whether the "in the name of Jesus" formula (or similar formulas—i.e., "in the name of Christ") invalidates a baptism. So the question becomes, "Is such a form valid?"

Biblically, there's nothing that helps us answer this question one way or the other. And, as mentioned above, even those places where it does speak of being baptized "in the name of Jesus," it's never in a context where this is clearly the *formula* used when administering the water.

Historically, it seems that such a formula was accepted as valid, at least during the reign of Pope Nicholas I in the ninth century. Here's what he had to say about it:

> You say that in your country many have been baptized by a certain Jew (you do not know whether he is Christian or pagan), and you are asking what should be done about them. If they truly baptized in the name of the Holy Trinity or *only in the name of Christ*, as we read in the Acts of the Apostles [2:38; 19:5] (for it is one and the same thing, as St. Ambrose explains), it is clear that they should not be baptized again.[181]

Perhaps this explains why the *Catechism* is guarded regarding the formula of baptism and says only what the formulas currently used in the Latin and Eastern liturgies are (both of which are trinitarian), without specifying that a trinitarian formula is necessary (1240). Furthermore, the *Code of Canon Law* doesn't even mention the formula at all and simply says, "Baptism is to be conferred either by immersion or by pouring; the prescripts of the conference of bishops are to be observed" (§854).

But there is a bit of a twist. A few hundred years before Pope Nicholas I, Pope Pelagius I, in his letter *Admonemus ut* to Bishop Gaudentius of Volterra (ca. 558–559), seems to have rejected the "in the name of Christ" formula. He writes,

> Concerning the heretics ... they assert that they were baptized only in the name of Christ and also with only one immersion, whereas the evangelical precept ... admonishes us to *administer each holy baptism in the name of the Trinity* and also by triple immersion, as our Lord, speaking to his disciples, said: "Go, baptize all nations *in the name of the Father and of the Son and of the Holy Spirit*" (Matt. 28:19).
>
> If, in fact, therefore, those among the aforesaid heretics ... should admit to having been *baptized only in the name of the Lord, you should, when they come to the Catholic faith, baptize them, without any uncertainty of doubt, in the name of the Holy Trinity.*
>
> If, however ... it becomes evident from a manifest confession that they have been baptized in the name of the Trinity, you will hasten to bring them into the Catholic faith making use only of the grace of the reconciliation accorded [them].[182]

Whenever we have something like this where there is uncertainty, we must look to most recent authoritative statements of the Magisterium. Fortunately, there is such a statement. In

2012, the Congregation for the Doctrine of the Faith (now called the Dicastery for the Doctrine of the Faith) published a document entitled "A New Response of the Congregation for the Doctrine of the Faith on the Validity of Baptism." In it, the Congregation states,

> Baptism conferred in the name of the Father, the Son, and the Holy Spirit conforms to the command of the Lord found at the end of Matthew's Gospel: "Go therefore and make disciples of all nations, baptizing them in the name of the Father and of the Son and of the Holy Spirit" (28:19). The Church has no right to change what Christ himself has instituted. *Therefore, any baptism is invalid when it does not contain the invocation of the Most Holy Trinity, with the distinct expression of the three Persons with their respective names.* Throughout the ages, the Magisterium of the Church has repeatedly taught that Christian baptism is administered in the name of the Father and of the Son and of the Holy Spirit.[183]

It's clear that the Congregation is ruling that any non-trinitarian form, such as the "in the name of Jesus" formula, is *not* valid (invalid).

The Congregation then goes on to list several magisterial documents in support:

> There is no need here to compile a complete list of the relevant magisterial documents; it may suffice to cite some of the more notable ones: the *Tomus Damasi* (382), the decretals *Desiderabilem mihi* of Pope Saint Gregory II (726) and *Sacris liminibus* of Pope Saint Zacharias (748), the chapter *De fide catholica* of the Fourth Lateran Council (1215), the constitution *Fidei catholicae* of the Council of Vienne (1312), the bull *Exsultate Deo* of the Council of

> Florence (1439), the decree *De sacramentis* of the Council of Trent (1547).[184]

The Congregation then concludes,

> The liturgical documents on the rite of baptism *do not offer alternatives* to the terms Father, Son and Holy Spirit.[185]

Some may argue that this document is speaking specifically of two different aberrations in the Church. And that is true. It was written in response to feminists who were using the forms of "in the name of the Creator, Redeemer, and Sanctifier" or, "Creator, Liberator, and Sustainer." Both are declared invalid by the Congregation.

But in the process of answering these errant formulations, the CDF makes the general statement that "any baptism is invalid when it does not contain the invocation of the Most Holy Trinity" and concludes that the liturgical documents offer no alternatives. This would seem to be in line with Pope Pelagius I above, as well as all the magisterial statements cited in the document.

Thus, it seems clear cut that according to current magisterial teaching—which, of course, carries weight only for Catholics—the Pentecostal Oneness baptism "in the name of Jesus" is considered invalid.

Conclusion

The trinitarian formula reveals to us the core truth of the sacrament of baptism, a truth proclaimed by St. Peter: "His divine power has granted to us all things that pertain to life and godliness, through the knowledge of him who called us to his own glory and excellence, by which he has granted to us his precious and very great promises, that through these you may escape from the corruption that is in the world because of passion, and *become partakers of the divine nature*" (2 Pet. 1:3–4). Such participation in the life of the Trinity is precisely what Jesus meant by the new birth in John 3:5—a life that is necessary for the kingdom of heaven. And baptism, administered using the trinitarian formula, is what gives us such life.

Part III

The Theology

CHAPTER 10

Salvation and Baptism

Throughout the book so far, we've given evidence *that* baptism saves. But when such a truth is proclaimed, many questions arise. For example, what's the extent of the effects of baptism? Does it extend to *all* sins, both original and personal? And does it extend to sins committed *after* baptism? Also, to what extent does baptism take care of punishments for sin?

Furthermore, if salvation is necessary for salvation, what happens to a person who dies without baptism, whether an adult or a child under the age of reason? Also, if we profess the belief that baptism saves, then how does that not take away from Jesus? For some Christians, the claim that baptism saves is problematic because it can take the focus off Jesus as our Savior.

In this chapter, we will take each of these questions in turn.

What Is the Scope of the Effects of Baptism?

The scope of the effects of baptism is very broad. The sacrament takes care of *all* sins, both original and personal. Also, it remits all *punishments* for sin, both temporal and eternal. The *Catechism* states as much:

> By baptism *all sins* are forgiven, original sin and all personal sins, as well as all punishment for sin. In those who have been reborn *nothing remains that would impede their entry into the kingdom of God*, neither Adam's sin,

> nor personal sin, *nor the consequences of sin*, the gravest of which is separation from God (1263).

Concerning the remission of all punishment due to sin, it's true that if someone were to steal money, repent, and get baptized, he may still have to pay back the money, supposing the one he stole from demands financial restitution. But, as the *Catechism* points out, "nothing remains that would impede their entry *into the kingdom of God*," like unhealthy attachments to creaturely goods or displeasure due to him for the sake of manifesting God's justice.

From this teaching it follows that anyone who dies immediately after receiving baptism goes straight to heaven—no need for purgatory. This is why some throughout Christian history prolonged their reception of baptism, hoping they could receive it right before death and bypass purgatory. Such a practice, however, is incompatible with God's will, as it presumes on God's grace. After all, the man who puts off baptism may not have the chance to receive it when the time comes! So everyone who is not baptized should be baptized as soon as he is able.

Now, the reason why the effect of baptism is plenary when it comes to sin and its punishment is that the baptized mystically enter the passion of Christ, which was sufficient for plenary satisfaction for sins. Rooted in St. Paul's baptismal theology in Romans 6:3-4, Aquinas articulates this rationale in the following manner:

> As the Apostle says (Romans 6:3-4), "all we who are baptized in Christ Jesus, are baptized in his death: for we are buried together with him, by baptism unto death"; which is to say that by baptism man is incorporated in the very death of Christ.
>
> Now it is manifest from what has been said above (III:48:4; III:49:3) that Christ's death satisfied sufficient-

> ly for sins, "not for ours only, but also for those of the whole world," according to 1 John 2:2. Consequently no kind of satisfaction should be enjoined on one who is being baptized, for any sins whatever: and this would be to dishonor the passion and death of Christ, as being insufficient for the plenary satisfaction for the sins of those who were to be baptized.[186]

So it's our full participation in Christ's passion that makes the sacrament of baptism have such plenary effects.

What about post-baptismal sins? Does baptism take care those, too? The answer is no. The sacrament of reconciliation takes care of such sins. The *Catechism* teaches in paragraph 1446 (emphasis added):

> Christ instituted the sacrament of penance for all sinful members of his Church: above all *for those who, since baptism, have fallen into grave sin*, and have thus lost their baptismal grace and wounded ecclesial communion. It is to them that *the sacrament of penance* offers a new possibility to convert and *to recover the grace of justification*. The Fathers of the Church present this sacrament as "*the second plank [of salvation]* after the shipwreck which is the loss of grace.

Therefore, although baptism has a plenary effect when received, it does not extend to sins committed afterward. Our Lord instituted confession for those sins, telling the apostles, "If you forgive the sins of any, they are forgiven; if you retain the sins of any, they are retained" (John 20:23).

What Happens to an Adult Who Dies Without Baptism?

As mentioned above, whenever baptism is spoken of as being salvific, questions arise as to whether people who die without baptism can be saved. Our answers to these questions depend on whether we're talking about people who have the use of reason or not. Given that there is a range of ages for those who have the use of reason (e.g., an eight-year-old child to an adult) and those who don't (e.g., a severely mentally handicapped person), let's specify, for the sake of simplicity, "adult" to mean those who have the use of reason and "infant" to mean those who don't.

Now, when it comes to "adults" dying without baptism, there are four possible candidates:

- Candidate A: an adult who died without baptism, knew about it, and rejected it
- Candidate B: an adult who died without baptism, knew about it, and consciously desired it
- Candidate C: an adult who died without baptism and didn't know about it, and such lack of knowledge *was* due to his own fault
- Candidate D: an adult who died without baptism and didn't know about it, and such lack of knowledge *wasn't* due to his own fault, and he had an unconscious or implicit desire for it, given his rightly ordered interior disposition toward truth and goodness

When it comes to the question of salvation, candidates A and C would be numbered among the damned. Concerning the person who knew about baptism and rejected it, the rationale for his damnation is that to reject the gift is to reject the gift-giver. The rationale for candidate C is that to be responsible for such lack of knowledge is a form of a positive rejection of the gift, and thereby the gift-giver.

Concerning candidates B and D, we can start with the Council of Trent. It infallibly teaches that "desire" suffices for receiving the graces of the sacraments in general. Canon four specifies:

> If anyone shall say, that the sacraments of the New Law are not necessary unto salvation, but superfluous, and that without them, *and without the desire thereof*, men, through faith alone, obtain of God the grace of justification; though all [the sacraments] be not necessary for every individual; let him be anathema.[187]

To state the above canon positively, the grace of justification can be obtained *at least* by a desire for the sacraments when they cannot be received in reality. Since one such sacrament is baptism, it follows that a person can obtain the grace of justification with a desire for baptism, even when the sacrament is not actually received. And given that an anathema is attached to it, this teaching is infallible.

Now, there is a counter to the above line of reasoning that we need to be aware of—a counter that I received back in 2023 while on *Catholic Answers Live*.[188] A gentleman called in to express his disagreement with my reading of the above canon. He countered that the phrase "without x and y" ("without them [the sacraments] and without the desire of them") doesn't mean having at least y ("the desire for the sacrament") is sufficient. For example, he went on to explain, the statement "a wedding cannot take place without a bride and a groom" doesn't mean that having at least a groom is sufficient for the wedding. Obviously, you need both!

Similarly, he argued, the meaning of Trent's "without the sacrament and the desire of them" formula is saying that to obtain the grace of justification, you need both the sacrament and the desire for it. In other words, you can't just go through the motions. A person (if the person is an adult) must intend to receive what the sacrament gives.

I'll admit that my response to his counter on the air wasn't as airtight as I would have liked it to be, given that I'd never heard this counter before and didn't have much time to think it through. This being the case, I thought it might be good to share a more thought-out response here.

The first thing to note is that the gentleman's example of a wedding, a bride, and a groom is correct. The statement "a wedding cannot take place without a bride and a groom" doesn't mean having at least the groom is sufficient. Rather, it means that you need both a bride and a groom to have a wedding.

As true as this may be, it doesn't mean Trent's use of the formula "without x and y" is meant to be interpreted in this way. Let me explain.

In the wedding example, the implied targeted question is whether a wedding can happen without a bride or a groom. Of course, the answer is no. You need both. This is why it is correct to interpret the above statement, "a wedding cannot happen without a bride and a groom," to mean you need both a bride and a groom to have a wedding.

Now, recall that the gentleman reads Trent's teaching—"without the sacraments and a desire for them"—to mean that we must have a desire for the sacrament when we receive the sacrament to obtain the grace of justification. On this reading, the implied targeted question is whether we can obtain the grace of justification by receiving the sacraments without a desire for them.

But here's the rub: the context of the canon shows that this is not the targeted question. The targeted question, rather, is whether the sacraments are necessary for salvation. The canon has in its sight some of the Reformers, who said and were saying the sacraments were not necessary for salvation and thereby superfluous. Note the canon's opening line: "If anyone shall say that the sacraments of the New Law are not necessary for salvation but are superfluous . . . let him be anathema."

Now, if you're a person who thinks the sacraments aren't necessary for salvation and thereby superfluous, then you're not going to think they're needed to obtain the grace of justification. Nor will you agree with the common theological tradition prior to and at the time of the council—namely, that one must have at least a desire for the sacraments when they are not actually received to obtain the grace of justification.[189]

Given that these are the logical consequences of thinking the sacraments aren't necessary for salvation, and that the targeted question of the canon is whether the sacraments are necessary for salvation, the formula "without the sacraments and a desire for them" fits best with the above twofold scenario: the actual reception of the sacraments and having a desire for them when they cannot be received actually in reality. This is far from the question of whether we must have a desire for the sacrament when we receive the sacrament.

Another response to the above counterargument is that the council, earlier in chapter four of its Decree on Justification, makes it explicit that the desire for baptism—in particular—suffices for salvation. It states,

> By which words a description of the justification of the impious is interwoven, to the effect that it is a translation from that state in which man is born a child of the first Adam, into the state of grace, and of the adoption of the sons of God, through the second Adam, Jesus Christ, our Savior. And this translation, since the gospel has been promulgated, cannot be effected, without the laver of regeneration, *or the desire thereof*, as it is written; Unless a man be born again of water and of the Holy Ghost, he cannot enter into the kingdom of God.[190]

Although I appreciate the challenge issued by the gentleman who called in, and I wish I could have offered a more pointed response at the time for our listeners and viewers, his counter simply doesn't succeed. Therefore, we're justified (pun intended) in reading the above canon, and chapter four of the Council of Trent's Decree on Justification, in a way that implies that Trent infallibly affirmed the teaching that the desire for the sacraments when they cannot be received actually in reality is sufficient to obtain the grace of justification (assuming that the sacraments are not available to be used).

The question now becomes whether the "desire" spoken of by Trent is explicit or implicit. *Explicit* desire would involve a conscious desire for the sacrament (candidate B above). *Implicit* desire refers to an individual who has a desire for God and what he has to offer us without having the relevant knowledge that baptism is something that God has to offer us for salvation (candidate D).

Given the tradition of the Church, it's reasonable to conclude that it's a reference to *explicit* desire. For example, it's found in the early Church Fathers. The main witnesses to this belief are Ss. Ambrose and Augustine. Ambrose mentions it in his funeral oration for the Emperor Valentine II, who died without baptism. Ambrose states,

> Should he not acquire the grace for which he longed? Certainly: As he desired it, he has attained it.... His pious desire has absolved him."[191]

Augustine follows suit:

> I find that not only suffering for the sake of Christ can replace that which is lacking in baptism, but also faith and conversion of the heart (*fidem conversionemque cordis*), if perhaps the shortness of the time does not permit the celebration of the mystery of baptism."[192]

This belief of baptism by explicit desire also has a pedigree in the tradition of scholasticism, with figures such as St. Bernard of Clairvaux, Hugo of St. Victor, and St. Thomas Aquinas defending it.[193]

We can also appeal to magisterial teaching on this front. Consider, for example, Pope Innocent II's letter *Apostolicam Sedem* to the bishop of Cremona.[194] He writes,

> The presbyter who, you said, ended [his] final days *without the water of baptism we declare without hesitation to have been freed from original sin and to have attained the joy of the heavenly fatherland since he persevered in the faith of Holy Mother Church and in the confession of Christ's name.*
>
> In addition, read in the eighth book of Augustine's *De civitate Dei*, where, among other things, it says: "Baptism is administered invisibly when it is impeded, not by the contempt of religion, but by the barrier of necessity." Likewise, go back to the book of blessed Ambrose, *De obitu valentiniani*, where he upholds the same thing.
>
> The questions having thus been put to rest. Hold to the judgments of the learned Fathers, and, in your church, ask that continual prayers and sacrifices be offered for the above-mentioned presbyter.[195]

Pope Innocent III (1198–1216) affirms the same belief in his letter *Debitum Officii Pontificalis* (The Duty of the Pontifical Office), written to the bishop of Metz. He's responding to an inquiry concerning a certain Jew who attempted to baptize himself using the trinitarian formula. Pope Innocent III responds,

> We respond that, since there should be a distinction between the one baptizing and the one baptized, as is clearly gathered from the words of the Lord, when he says to

> the apostles, "Go baptize all nations in the name etc." (cf. Matt. 28:19), the Jew mentioned must be baptized again by another, that it may be shown that he who is baptized is one person, and he who baptizes another. . . .
>
> If, however, such a one had died immediately, he would have rushed to his heavenly home without delay *because of the faith of the sacrament, although not because of the sacrament of faith.*[196]

Notice that Pope Innocent III affirms that this unnamed Jew would have achieved salvation without the sacrament by the faith he exercised in his explicit desire to receive it.

The *Catechism* doesn't break with this tradition, but rather carries it on, stating succinctly,

> For catechumens [those who are seeking baptism] who die before their baptism, their *explicit desire to receive it*, together with repentance for their sins, and charity, *assures them the salvation* that they were not able to receive through the sacrament (1259).

The same line of reasoning applies to martyrs who die without baptism. They undergo what the Church calls the "baptism of blood" (CCC 1258). These people are "baptized by their death for and with Christ" and thus receive "the fruits of baptism without being a sacrament."

Everything that we've said so far pertains to an *explicit* desire for baptism. But what about what theologians call an *implicit* desire? An implicit desire for baptism would be a desire a person has for it without knowing it. How does this play out?

Let's say, for example, a person has an interior desire to know and receive all the gifts that God has revealed. Yet this person, for whatever reason, doesn't know about the sacrament of baptism. *And* his lack of knowledge is due to no fault of his own.

Given that this person desires all the gifts God has given, and baptism is such a gift, it follows that this person would have an implicit desire for baptism, since baptism is a gift of God.

Our question now is, "Can such a desire be sufficient for salvation?"

We have precedent for it in the teaching of Jesus. Consider what he teaches in Mark 9:38–40:

> John said to him, "Teacher, we saw a man casting out demons in your name, and we forbade him, because he was not following us." But Jesus said, "Do not forbid him; for no one who does a mighty work in my name will be able soon after to speak evil of me. For he that is not against us is for us. For truly, I say to you, whoever gives you a cup of water to drink because you bear the name of Christ, will by no means lose his reward.

This implication of the passage is clear: Someone who is not within the visible boundaries of the community of the faithful can be moved by the Spirit to do mighty deeds.

Now, Jesus goes beyond the mere performance of mighty deeds by someone outside the visible boundaries of the community. He highlights, so it seems, the interior state of such a person.

Notice that Jesus says of the person who was driving out demons in his name, "No one who does a mighty work in my name will be able soon after to *speak evil of me*." This implies that the individual is, at least in his heart and mind, ordered toward the Lord. And Jesus confirms this in the next statement: "For he who is not against us is for us." To be *for the Lord* is to have an interior disposition that constitutes a state of justice, or being saved.

So Jesus reveals someone can be invisibly united to him and the community of the faithful even though he is not united visibly—that's to say, he's not formally a member of the community. This is the essence of what we mean by "implicit desire."

To complement the above scriptural basis, we also have magisterial teaching. Take, for example, Pope Pius IX's *On Promotion of False Doctrines* (1863). Although he doesn't teach on the implicit desire for baptism explicitly, what he says provides support for it. He writes,

> It is ... necessary to mention and censure a very grave error entrapping some Catholics who believe that it is possible to arrive at eternal salvation although living in error and alienated from the true faith and Catholic unity. Such belief is certainly opposed to Catholic teaching. There are, of course, those who are *struggling with invincible ignorance* about our most holy religion. Sincerely *observing the natural law and its precepts* inscribed by God on all hearts and ready to obey God, they *live honest lives and are able to attain eternal life by the efficacious virtue of divine light and grace.* Because God knows, searches and clearly understands the minds, hearts, thoughts, and nature of all, his supreme kindness and clemency do not permit anyone at all who is not guilty of deliberate sin to suffer eternal punishments.[197]

Pope Pius XII goes one step further and explicitly connects the above rationale with the idea of having an implicit desire for baptism. Here's what he teaches in his 1943 encyclical *Mystici Corporis*:

> We have committed to the protection and guidance of heaven those who do not belong to the visible body of the Catholic Church.... *For even though by an unconscious desire and longing they have a certain relationship*

> *with the mystical body of the Redeemer*, they still remain deprived of those many heavenly gifts and helps which can only be enjoyed in the Catholic Church. Therefore may they enter into Catholic unity and, joined with us in the one, organic body of Jesus Christ, may they together with us run on to the one Head in the society of glorious love.[198]

Pius XII makes explicit that someone can have an "unconscious desire and longing" to be united to the Church, and by virtue of that desire, such an individual can be *factually* united to it. From here it follows that if such a person were to die in this unity with the Church, he would be saved, even though he hadn't been baptized. The reason is that union with the Church, and thereby union with Christ who is head of the Church, is that which guarantees us final salvation after death.

The Second Vatican Council preserved this tradition in its Dogmatic Constitution on the Church *Lumen Gentium* (1964). It teaches,

> Those who, through no fault of their own, do not know the gospel of Christ or his Church, but who nevertheless seek God with a sincere heart, and, moved by grace, try in their actions to do his will as they know it through the dictates of their conscience—those too may achieve eternal salvation (16).

It's true that this passage doesn't use the language of "implicit desire." However, the teaching describes the reality: "With a sincere heart . . . do [God's] will as they know it through the dictates of their conscience."

Like what Pius XII did with Pius IX's teaching above, the *Catechism* connects this teaching from *Lumen Gentium*, which in essence is the same as Pius IX's teaching, to the idea of having an implicit desire for baptism: "It may be supposed that such persons would have desired baptism explicitly if they had known its necessity" (1260).

The rationale behind all the above magisterial statements about people who die without baptism is that the necessity of baptism for salvation applies to "those to whom the gospel has been proclaimed and who have had the possibility of asking for this sacrament" (CCC 1257). Again, "God has bound salvation to the sacrament of Baptism, but he himself is not bound by his sacraments."[199]

Now, everything that we've said here doesn't mean the Catholic Church and the sacraments, and in particular the sacrament of baptism, are not important. They are. Jesus started the Catholic Church, and he gave us the seven sacraments. Therefore, out of love for Christ, it's necessary that we belong to his Church and receive his sacraments.

Moreover, when it comes to the question of salvation, anyone who is saved is saved by virtue of his union with the Catholic Church, even if such a union is only invisible. The *Catechism* teaches as much in paragraph 846 (emphasis added):

> How are we to understand this affirmation ["There is No Salvation Outside the Church"], often repeated by the Church Fathers? Re-formulated positively, it means that all salvation comes from Christ the head *through the Church* which is his body.

Thus, the affirmation that an implicit desire is sufficient for salvation doesn't entail religious indifferentism. When properly understood, both the sufficiency of an implicit desire and the necessity to believe in the Catholic faith can be affirmed at the same time.

What Happens to an Infant Who Dies Without Baptism?

With our question about the fate of those adults who die without baptism answered, we now turn to the question concerning the fate of infants who die without baptism. The Church gives no definitive teaching on the matter. However, the Church does permit theological opinions on the fate of unbaptized infants.

Traditionally, schools of theology favored the idea of *limbo*, a postmortem state of existence that includes the souls of infants who die without baptism and thus with original sin only. Such souls wouldn't experience the torments of the damned, but they also wouldn't be able to experience the beatific vision due to original sin.[200]

The International Theological Commission pointed out in its 2007 document "The Hope of Salvation for Infants Who Die Without Being Baptized" (approved by Pope Benedict XVI) that the theory of limbo "never entered into the dogmatic definitions of the Magisterium." However, it did occupy a status of "ordinary teaching" or "common teaching," which is a non-infallible category of official Church teaching.

For example, when the Jansenists rejected Augustine's view of limbo, the popes of the time—Paul III, Benedict XIV, and Clement XIII—came to the defense of the idea.[201] Pope Pius VI, in his papal bull *Auctorem Fidei*, condemned as "false, rash, and injurious to the Catholic schools" the Jansenist rejection of limbo as a "Pelagian fable."[202]

The Commission summarizes the Magisterium's history on this issue as follows:

> In summary: The affirmation that infants who die without baptism suffer the privation of the beatific vision has long been the common doctrine of the Church, which

> must be distinguished from the faith of the Church. As for the theory that the privation of the beatific vision is their sole punishment, to the exclusion of any other pain, this is a theological opinion, despite its long acceptance in the West. The particular theological thesis concerning a "natural happiness" sometimes ascribed to these infants likewise constitutes a theological opinion.[203]

Neither the Second Vatican Council nor the *Catechism of the Catholic Church* mentions limbo. In fact, when the *Catechism* addresses the fate of unbaptized infants specifically, it noticeably ignores the issue (1261).

The current Magisterium, though it doesn't reject the theory of limbo, does offer a supplement, or even an alternative, to it. The position that the *Catechism* takes is one of humility. It states that "the Church can only entrust" these infants "to the mercy of God." However, the *Catechism* does express hope "that there is a way of salvation for [these] children" because of two things: 1) God's desire that all men should be saved (1 Tim. 2:4) and 2) Jesus' tenderness toward children (Mark 10:14).

Does this mean that we can rest assured that unbaptized babies who die go straight to heaven? By no means! Rather, the authors of the *Catechism*, hopeful but humble, and moved by the love that Jesus has for children, make this exhortation: "All the more urgent is the Church's call not to prevent little children coming to Christ through the gift of holy baptism."

What About the Concern of the Ritual Taking Our Focus Off Jesus?

There's one last question that we need to address concerning the belief that baptism saves. For some Christians, the claim that baptism saves is problematic because it can take the focus off Jesus as our Savior. Take Gavin Ortlund, for example. In his dialogue with apologist Trent Horn, he expresses this concern in the following way:

> My honest, sincere, heart-level concern is something that happens so much that I think that baptismal regeneration traditions can push against. So I'm not saying this always must happen for anyone who affirms baptismal regeneration, but what I just honestly see so much at the street level is a formalism where the focus is put on the rite.
>
> It's like, "Baptism saved me, so I'm good." And there isn't what you've mentioned: the need for faith. . . . The whole point is to point our eyes to Jesus Christ. Can you understand this, the worry here of, at least at street-level practice, traditions that think it's baptism that causes regeneration, can put so much focus on the right, that we get stuck there? We're not looking from it, up to Christ.[204]

Ortlund expresses a legitimate concern here. *Anyone* who focuses on the ritual of a sacrament to the exclusion of Jesus Christ would need to be corrected and invited to a true understanding. However, Ortlund appeals to this concern as reason to reject the belief that baptism saves. That's what the entire dialogue is about. And it's this inference that is problematic.

First, why should we reject the belief that baptism saves simply because *some* people *mistakenly* focus on the rite over, above, and before Jesus Christ? We don't reject interpreting Scripture just because some people mistakenly interpret it to their own destruction (see 2 Pet. 3:15–16). Nor do we reject the practice of religion simply because some who practice it do so in a way that leads to unjust conflict and violence.

Concerning the interpretation of the scriptures, we realize that it's not the interpretation of Scripture *itself* that leads to destruction. Rather, it's specific interpretations and whatever method the interpreter is using. Similarly, when it comes to religion, we recognize that it's not religion *itself* that leads to conflict and violence. Rather, it's the perversion of religion by the one causing unjust conflict and violence.

The same line of reasoning applies to those who focus on the baptismal ritual in the place of Christ. Ortlund, or anyone, for that matter, shouldn't reject the belief that baptism saves on these grounds, because it's not the belief that baptism saves that is the problem. Rather, it's the lack of love for Christ on the part of the one who approaches the waters of baptism, whether that's due to his own fault or not. There are countless people who *do* approach the waters of baptism with a deep love for Christ.

So the concern that Ortlund expresses here has no bearing on whether the belief that baptism saves is true. It's simply *a* concern, but it's not necessarily a concern about the *belief itself*.

Second, Ortlund's logic works against his own view. Ortlund affirms that baptism gives grace—a grace that increases one's sanctity after the initial grace of salvation has been given—but denies that baptism gives the initial grace of *salvation*, professing that baptism merely symbolizes it. He articulates this view in his online video entitled "Baptismal Regeneration: Responding to Common Arguments." He states,

> So if we were to make a distinction here between the grace by which God brings us into a state of salvation and the grace by which God nourishes and strengthens and furthers us in our salvation, the Baptist tradition puts baptism in the latter category. It's not the cause [of salvation].[205]

Wouldn't it be possible that someone from Ortlund's congregation approach the waters of baptism focusing solely on the ritual as the source of grace rather than Jesus? Sure, it would. And that's a legitimate concern. But based on the logic embedded within Ortlund's challenge, he would have to reject his own belief articulated above. Therefore, his expressed concern is self-defeating.

Although Ortlund's concern is valid, it's no reason to reject the belief that baptism saves. Potential abuse is not a reason to reject legitimate use.

Conclusion

It's one thing to give evidence that baptism saves. But it's another to answer all the theological questions that such a belief gives rise to. In this chapter, we've answered some of those most pressing questions.

We saw that the scope of baptism extends to *all* sin and *all* sin's punishments, applying the full measure of the merits won for us through Jesus' death on the cross. We saw that an adult can possibly be saved without the sacrament of baptism on account of either an explicit or implicit desire for baptism. Concerning infants who die without baptism, we saw that the Church exercises humility in acknowledging its uncertainty. Yet it gives us reason to hope that infants who die without baptism receive the saving grace of baptism.

Finally, we saw that there is no good reason to reject the belief that baptism saves on account of some people who make the ritual their sole focus instead of Jesus. Although this is a legitimate concern, it has no bearing on whether the belief is true or not.

There are other theological questions that arise in discussions about baptism—precisely those that pertain to faith and its relation to the sacrament. Our next chapter will deal with such questions.

Chapter 11

Faith and Baptism

In our chapter on infant baptism, one of the objections posed was that infants can't exercise faith. This objection stems from the belief that the Bible reveals that faith is necessary for salvation, and from Jesus' explicit teaching that he who believes and is baptized is saved (Matt. 16:16).

We met the apologetical requirements by showing why such an objection has no force against the belief and practice of infant baptism. But there are a few theological questions that remain concerning the relation between faith and baptism. It's these sorts of questions that we will address in this chapter.

Is Faith Necessary for Baptism?

The first question is whether faith is in fact necessary for baptism. The answer is yes. The *Catechism* teaches that "baptism is the sacrament of faith" (1253) and thus connected with faith (1226). This belief is rooted in Jesus' command, "he who believes and is baptized will be saved; but he who does not believe will be condemned" (Mark 16:16).

However, we must distinguish between faith that precedes baptism and faith that's received with sanctification in baptism. Concerning the latter, which is referred to as the *theological* virtue of faith, it's a faith that justifies.[206] This is so because baptismal faith is animated by charity. Theologians call this kind of faith *fides formata*—formed faith (formed by charity).[207]

The Council of Trent teaches that "faith, unless hope and charity be added to it, neither unites one perfectly with Christ, nor makes him a living member of his body."[208] "This faith," the council goes on, "catechumens [people preparing to be baptized] beg of the Church before the sacrament of baptism, when they ask for 'faith which bestows life eternal,' which without hope and charity faith cannot bestow."[209] So faith—*fides formata*—is necessary for baptism in that it is necessary for baptism to produce the grace of salvation.[210] Such faith is not merited, but is a gift from God. It is the faith that, according to Paul, justifies us (see Rom. 3:28).

There's another kind of faith that's necessary for baptism: a faith that *precedes* baptism. This faith, too, is a gift from God,[211] but it is *not* formed or vivified by charity. Consequently, it doesn't justify, but *precedes* justification.

Theologians call this kind of faith *fides informis* (non-formed faith).[212] The *Catechism* describes it as "not a perfect and mature faith, but a beginning that is called to develop" (1253). It remains inefficacious until perfected in baptism by charity.

According to the Council of Trent, the purpose of this faith is to *dispose* the soul for justification. The council states,

> Now they are disposed to that justice [cans. 7 and 9] when, aroused and assisted by divine grace, receiving faith "by hearing" [Rom. 10:17], they are freely moved toward God, believing that to be true which has been divinely revealed and promised [can. 12 and 14], and this especially, that the sinner is justified by God through his grace.[213]

This kind of faith is also expressed by people in the Bible when they respond to the apostolic call to repentance. Take, for example, the Philippian jailer in Acts 16. When he asks Paul, "What must I do to be saved?" (v. 30), Paul responds, "*Believe* in the Lord Jesus, and you will be saved." Luke then tells us that Paul baptized the jailer and his family: "And [the jailer] was baptized at once, with all his family" (v. 33). The assumption is that the jailer believed.

Both kinds of faith, therefore, are necessary for baptism according to how each relates to the sacrament. One predisposes for the sacrament, and the other is given in the sacrament, which in turn brings about the grace of salvation.

Why Get Baptized If Someone Can Have Saving Faith Before Baptism?

In our above answers, we distinguished between *justifying* or *saving* faith and a faith that doesn't save. But in the previous chapter, we said that it's possible for someone to be saved without the sacrament of baptism, which seemingly would entail that in principle, it's possible for someone to receive the gift of justifying or saving faith prior to reception of the sacrament.

Now, if that's the case, then the question arises: "Why get baptized?" The belief that justifying faith can be given without the sacrament seemingly makes baptism superfluous.

Our answer to this question is threefold. First, we can never be absolutely sure, in a particular case, whether God in fact communicates the grace of salvation without the sacrament. Second, obeying God's command to be baptized gives him glory. God wills baptism to be the ordinary means through which he communicates the grace of salvation. Consequently, when we get baptized we manifest God's divine plan, and thereby his divine wisdom, even if he wills to communicate such grace in other ways in extraordinary cases. There's nothing superfluous about manifesting the divine glory.

Third, St. Thomas Aquinas speculates that there is a *spiritual* benefit to receiving the sacrament versus not, even though an individual can be saved by justifying faith in either case. The benefit is a *complete* remission of punishment, whether temporal or eternal, due for sin. We touched on this in the previous chapter, but Aquinas applies it directly to this question. He writes,

> As stated above (Article 1, Reply to Objection 2; III:68:2) man receives the forgiveness of sins before baptism in so far as he has baptism of desire, explicitly or implicitly; and yet when he actually receives baptism, he *receives a fuller remission, as to the remission of the entire punishment.*[214]

Aquinas goes on to give Cornelius and his Gentile friends in Acts 10 as an example. He acknowledges that they are saved prior to receiving baptism, which means they receive the gift of justifying faith (faith informed by charity) without the sacrament. But when they receive baptism at Peter's prompting, "they receive yet a greater fullness of grace and virtues,"[215] which, for Aquinas, would be the full remission of the debt of temporal punishment for sin.

Concerning someone who dies without the sacrament but has a desire for it, whether explicitly or implicitly, Aquinas speculates that some *temporal* punishment for sin might remain:

> Suppose, therefore, a catechumen to have the desire for baptism (else he could not be said to die in his good works, which cannot be without "faith that worketh by charity"). Such a one, were he to die, would not forthwith come to eternal life, but *would suffer punishment for his past sins*—"but he himself shall be saved, yet so as by fire," as is stated in 1 Corinthians 3:15.[216]

So, given what we've said above, the belief that someone can be saved by justifying faith without the sacrament of baptism doesn't make baptism superfluous. Given this order of providence, we give God glory by using the sacrament that he's given us—and, perhaps, we wouldn't have the full remission of the debt of temporal punishment for sin without the sacrament.

Chapter 12

The Baptismal Seal and the Institution of Baptism

When it comes to the theology of baptism, it's a bit of a mixed bag concerning the level of certainty we have about things. Above, I mentioned that the Church bows in humility concerning what happens to infants who die without baptism. Two other items in the mixed theological bag are the "baptismal seal" (CCC 1272) and the *institution* of baptism. Each is a mixed bag when it comes to theological certainty because on one level, both are infallibly taught by the Church. The "baptismal seal" is a real spiritual gift that baptism brings about within the soul. And baptism was really *instituted* by Christ as a saving sacrament.

However, there are several details about these items that fall within the category of speculative theology—things that we're not so sure about.

Let's start with the "baptismal seal," also called "the indelible spiritual mark" (CCC 1273). This mark—understood by many theologians to be a supernatural quality of the soul[217]—configures the baptized to Christ as a member of his mystical body and constitutes the believer as *belonging* to Christ (1272). It is *indelible* in that no sin can ever remove it, even if sin impedes baptism from bearing the fruits of salvation. The permanence of this seal also explains why baptism cannot be repeated.

The purpose of the seal is to confer full power upon the baptized to perform acts of Christian worship. As Aquinas teaches, just as "a coin is marked for use in exchange of goods, and soldiers are marked with a character as being deputed to military service," so too "each of the faithful is deputed [by the spiritual mark] to receive, or to bestow on others, things pertaining to the worship of God."[218]

The Council of Trent infallibly affirmed the existence of this sacramental spiritual character against those who denied it during the Reformation: "If anyone shall say that in the three sacraments—to wit, baptism, confirmation, and orders—there is not imprinted on the soul a character—that is, a certain spiritual and indelible sign, on account of which they cannot be repeated—let him be anathema."[219]

Scripture doesn't explicitly refer to the baptismal seal. However, there are a few passages that theologians have appealed to throughout the centuries. Take, for example, 2 Corinthians 1:21-22, where Paul writes, "It is God who establishes us with you in Christ, and has commissioned us; he has put *his seal upon us* and given us his Spirit in our hearts as a guarantee." Similarly, Paul writes to the Ephesians, "In him you also, who have heard the word of truth, the gospel of your salvation, and have believed in him, *were sealed* with the promised Holy Spirit" (Eph. 1:13). The ambiguity is whether these texts refer to the distinct effect of the character or simply grace itself.

This impression of a divine seal in baptism was also taught by a few of the Church Fathers. St. Cyril of Jerusalem, for example, teaches, "Following upon our faith, we receive like him *the spiritual seal*, being circumcised by the Holy Spirit *through baptism*, not in the foreskin of the body, but in the heart."[220] In the prologue to his lectures, he calls baptism "a holy indissoluble seal,"[221] and then again, in lecture seventeen, a "heavenly and sacred seal."[222] In lecture sixteen, he states that God "to this day seals the souls in baptism."[223]

St. Augustine would be the first to speak of the seal as a "character" conferred independently from grace. Ludwig Ott explains Augustine's treatment of the issue as follows:

> [According to] St. Augustine[,] all the essential characteristics of the sacramental character appear:
>
> a) Its differentiation and the separability from grace ("*consecratio*" in contra-distinction to "sanctification" or "*vitae aeternae participatio*"; Ep. 98, 5; De bapt. V 24, 34);
>
> b) The impossibility of losing it (C. ep. Parm. II 13, 29; C. litt. Petil. II 104, 239);
>
> c) As a consequence of the foregoing the impossibility of repeating the sacrament (C. ep. Parm. II 13, 28).[224]

Now, there are a few questions that arise concerning this seal. One is whether the seal remains after death. This is uncertain. The Church teaches that the seal is "indelible," as the above quote from the Council of Trent states. But it's unclear whether this pertains to this life alone or extends into the next.[225]

Some of the early Fathers and Scholastic theologians did favor the view that the mark endures into the afterlife. For example, Cyril taught that the "seal of the Holy Spirit" is "indelible throughout all ages."[226] Aquinas roots the eternal duration of the seal in the eternality of Christ's priesthood and the immortality of the soul.[227]

But this would not be of necessity. As stated above, the seal is ordered to those things "pertaining to the worship of God."[228] But, seemingly, Aquinas teaches that such worship is "the worship of the Church that now is."[229] Since the worship of the blessed in the afterlife is not the "worship of the

Church that now is"—that's to say, the worship on *this* side of the veil—there doesn't seem to be any necessity for the sacramental seal to endure after death.

Another question that pertains to the seal is whether someone who dies without the sacrament receives the character. We know that such a person can receive the grace of salvation. But when it comes to the character, it doesn't seem to be the case.

When the *Catechism* talks about the "baptism of blood," for example, it states that such a baptism, like the desire for baptism, "brings about the fruits of baptism *without being a sacrament*" (1258). The implication seems to be that something is given in the sacrament that is not given in the baptism of blood. What might that be? The baptismal seal.

The *Catechism* teaches in paragraph 1121 that the "seal" is a "*sacramental* character." In other words, it's a fruit that's given *insofar as* it's a *sacrament*. As Aquinas states, "the sacramental character is a thing as regards the exterior sacrament."[230] Given that the baptism of blood is *not* a sacrament, it would seem to follow that the seal is not given in the baptism of blood.

Another possible rationale as to why the seal wouldn't be given to someone who, although saved, dies without the sacrament is that the seal, as stated above, is ordered to Christian worship in the Church "as it now is."[231] If the departed soul can no longer participate in the Church's liturgical worship in this life, then, seemingly, there would be no need for the sacramental character.

With our reflection on the baptismal seal now complete, let's now turn to the *institution* of baptism. As I said, *that* Christ instituted baptism as the ordinary means through which we're initially saved is infallibly taught by the Church. But there are some things about the institution of baptism that we're not so sure about, like the *timing* of the sacrament's institution. This is a question that remains open. Theologians are divided in their opinions on the matter because it can't be established on the grounds of the Bible or Church teaching. The Bible doesn't tell us one way or the other, and the Church has never made any pronouncement on it.

Some theologians, including Aquinas, argue that Christ instituted the sacrament with his baptism in the Jordan.[232] This position, at least for some time in Church history, did have magisterial backing in the *Catechism of the Council of Trent*.[233]

Others, however, say Jesus instituted the sacrament in his conversation with Nicodemus.[234] Still others say it didn't happen until Jesus, right before he ascended, gave the mandate for the apostles to baptize (Matt. 28:19).[235]

Although these views seem probable, theologians have pointed out some of their problems.[236] A significant problem with the first opinion is that Scripture is completely silent. There is nothing in the Bible to suggest that Jesus' baptism was the moment when Christ *instituted* the sacrament of baptism. It may reveal some things about the sacrament (e.g., it opens heaven to us, the Trinity dwells in us, we enter filial relation with the Father, etc.), but such things don't prove that Christ *instituted* the sacrament at that time.

A problem with the second opinion is external circumstances of Jesus' conversation with Nicodemus. It's unbefitting that Jesus would institute such an important sacrament in the darkness of night with only one disciple. Furthermore, Jesus speaks of the necessity of the sacrament for salvation only, *without* giving any indication that he's making it binding from then on.

The third opinion—that Christ instituted the sacrament with the mandate for the apostles to make disciples by baptizing the nations—is viewed by some as most probable.[237] Nevertheless, this view is not conclusive, because such a mandate doesn't rule out an earlier institution.

St. Bonaventure was unique in his approach. He sought to bring together all the above opinions into a single explanation. Ludwig Ott articulates Bonaventure's approach as follows:

> St. Bonaventure (Com. In Ioan. c. 3. n. 19) seeks to unify the various opinions in the following fashion. According to the matter (*materialiter*) baptism was instituted when Christ was baptized; according to the form (*formaliter*) when he rose from the dead and gave the form (Matt. 28:19); according to the effect (*effective*), when he suffered, for it received its power from the Passion; according to the purpose (*finaliter*), when he foretold its necessity and its benefit (John 3:5).[238]

Given everything that we've said above, we can only conclude that the question as to when Christ instituted the sacrament of baptism remains an open one. We simply wait to see if the Church one day decides to settle it. Until then, we can only speculate.

Conclusion

The "baptismal seal" and the institution of baptism are a bit of mixed bag when it comes to definitive Church teaching. *That* the baptized receive such a baptismal seal is indeed infallible. Also, we know for sure that Christ instituted the sacrament.

But when it comes to some theological questions that such infallible beliefs give rise to, we're in the realm of speculative theology. Nevertheless, such things are good to reflect on because they keep our focus on the mysteries of God. As St. Paul writes, "set your minds on things that are above, not on things that are on earth" (Col. 3:2).

Part IV

The Life of the Baptized

Chapter 13

The Implications of Baptism for the Christian Life

There are seven implications that baptism has for our lives as a Christian, each of which arises from a particular dimension of the sacrament.

First, we must daily respond to God and his Word in *faith*. As we mentioned in a previous chapter, baptism is "the sacrament of faith" (CCC 1253), which gives us entrance into "the life of faith" (1236). "Faith," as defined by the *Catechism*, "is the theological virtue by which we believe in God and believe all that he has said and revealed to us, and that Holy Church proposes for our belief" (1814). Baptism, as "a sacrament of faith," thrusts us into a life in which we must *continually* profess our belief in God, his revelation, and infallible Church teaching. Such professions of faith can be as simple as "Jesus, I believe in you. Help my unbelief!"

Second, we must daily renounce Satan and his evil ways. Baptism not only signifies liberation from sin and the devil, but also brings about such liberation within us. This is why, during the baptismal ritual, the celebrant prays one or more prayers of exorcism over the candidate, and the candidate explicitly renounces Satan. (See baptismal promises below.) For a Christian to live out his baptism means to live his life free from the dominion of sin and the devil, which involves *continually* renouncing Satan and having recourse to the means that Christ has given us to set us free from post-baptismal sin: the sacrament of reconciliation.

Third, we must do the things that go with our new threefold role. The anointing with sacred chrism in baptism signifies the anointing that the baptized receives by the Holy Spirit, an anointing that makes the baptized a priest, prophet, and king in Christ (CCC 1241). A priest is one who offers sacrifice and prays on behalf of the people of God. As members of the universal priesthood of Christ (1268), we must offer our lives to God as living sacrifices (Rom. 12:1) and engage in intercessory prayer (1 Tim. 2:1-2).

A prophet is one who announces the truth about God and his revelation. Given that baptism constitutes us as prophets in Christ, we are mandated to announce the truth about God and his revelation: "Go therefore and make disciples . . . teaching them to observe all that I have commanded you" (Matt. 28:19-20).

A king is one who governs, and a good king governs wisely, which involves directing things to their proper goals or ends. As participants in the kingly role of Christ, we must direct our lives to our ultimate life's goal or end: union with God in heaven.

Fourth, we must daily conform our lives to Christ. In the baptismal ritual, the newly baptized ordinarily receives a white garment. As the *Catechism* states, this symbolizes that the baptized person has, in the words of St. Paul, "put on Christ" (1243, quoting Gal. 3:27). Now, to "put on Christ" means to conform our hearts and minds to the heart and mind of Christ. This means that we must daily think with and like Christ and make choices that are in conformity with what Christ wills for us.

Fifth, we must daily participate in the apostolic and missionary activity of the Church, in some way, shape, or form, according to our state in life. In the baptismal ritual, the newly baptized receives a candle, lit from the Easter candle, which signifies that the baptized person has been conformed to Christ to be "the light of the world" (Matt. 5:14; see also CCC 1243). To be a light to the world means to tell the world about the good that Jesus has done for us in our lives. As St. Peter writes, "[you are] God's own people, that you may declare the wonderful deeds of him who called you out of darkness into his marvelous light" (1 Pet. 2:9).

This is also due to our being "reborn as sons of God." The *Catechism* states,

> "Reborn as sons of God," [the baptized] must profess before men the faith they have received from God through the Church [*Lumen Gentium* 11] and participate in the apostolic and missionary activity of the people of God (1270).

Sixth, we must participate in the liturgical life of the Church, the most important part of which is Holy Mass. As we mentioned in the previous chapter, baptism imparts to the baptized "the sacramental character," also known as the "sacramental seal," which "consecrates [the baptized] for Christian religious worship" (CCC 1273)—in particular, "the holy liturgy of the Church." If the whole purpose of the sacramental character is to make us fit to participate in the liturgical life of the Church, then being faithful to our baptism necessarily entails participating in the liturgical life of the Church.

What's all this for? The answer constitutes our seventh and final implication: It's for the sake of obtaining the reward of eternal life. The *Catechism* puts it succinctly:

> The faithful Christian who has "kept the seal" until the end, remaining faithful to the demands of his baptism,

> will be able to depart this life "marked with the sign of faith," with his baptismal faith, in expectation of the blessed vision of God—the consummation of faith—and in the hope of resurrection (1274).

There's one last thing: To live out the demands of your baptism, you must first *recall* the demands of your baptism. So here are the baptismal promises that either you made yourself (if you were baptized after the age of reason) or that your parents made on your behalf:

- I renounce sin, so as to live in the freedom of the children of God.
- I renounce the lure of evil, so that sin may have no mastery over me.
- I renounce Satan, the author and prince of sin.
- I believe in God, the Father Almighty, Creator of heaven and earth.
- I believe in Jesus Christ, his only Son, our Lord, who was born of the Virgin Mary, suffered death and was buried, rose again from the dead and is seated at the right hand of the Father. I believe in the Holy Spirit, the holy Catholic Church, the communion of saints, the forgiveness of sins, the resurrection of the body, and life everlasting.

Being faithful to our baptism entails the reward of eternal life. This is part and parcel of the Christian life, which is the life of the baptized.

Chapter 14

The Significance of Baptism and Our Relation to the Church

Just as baptism has implications for our everyday lives as Christians, baptism also has implications for us *in relation to the Church*. Consider, for example, how we said in a previous question that baptism is "the door which gives access to the other sacraments" (CCC 1213).

In baptizing people, the Church, as a mother, offers to us, her newborn spiritual children, opportunities to stay close to her and grow in holiness. The other sacraments, and the access that baptism gives to them, represents the Church's motherly care. Just as a natural mother looks out for the physical well-being of her children, the Church looks out for our spiritual well-being.

Through baptism, therefore, we become related to the Church as children to a mother, and we're invited to stay close to her by receiving the other sacraments that she has to offer, especially the sacraments of confession, the Eucharist, and confirmation, and, when needed, anointing of the sick. Holy matrimony and holy orders depend on one's state in life. Baptism initiates our relation to the Church; the other sacraments sustain it.

Baptism also relates us to the Church insofar as it imparts to us the gift of faith. Faith is not something that we can hold on to all by ourselves. We received it within the Church community, and thus it can survive only within the Church community. The *Catechism* explains it this way: "Baptism is the sacrament of faith. But faith needs the community of believers. It is *only within the faith of the Church* that each of the faithful can believe" (1253, emphasis added).

This is not at all different from the reception and sustenance of our natural life. We received natural life within a community—the communion of our mother and father, along with those who support them—and our natural life could not have continued without the continued support of such a human community.

Not only is the Church necessary for us to receive and keep the gift of faith, but the Church is also necessary for our faith to grow. As the *Catechism* states, "for all the baptized, children or adults, faith must *grow* after baptism" (1254, emphasis added). Given what we said above, it's clear that we need the Church, and the sacraments that it offers us, to *grow* our faith as well.

There's one more aspect to consider with regard to the gift of faith and our relation to the Church: our share in the Church's mission to profess the Faith. In our previous chapter, we talked about how baptism imposes upon us the obligation to be witnesses to Jesus in the world. The same idea applies here, but the focus here is *the relation we have with the Church* in fulfilling our role to testify about the faith that we have received. Here's how the *Catechism* puts it: "'Reborn as sons of God, [the baptized] must profess before men the faith they have received from God through the Church' and participate in the apostolic and missionary activity of the people of God" (1270). Being faithful to our baptism, therefore, entails being faithful to the apostolic and missionary endeavors of the Church.

Finally, baptism has implications for our relation to the Church insofar as we become subject to the leaders of the Church (the pope and bishops and priests in union with him). This is rooted in the Bible: "Obey your leaders and submit to them; for they are keeping watch over your souls" (Heb. 13:17).

Such oversight belongs to official Church leaders (pope, bishops, and priests) by divine prerogative. Jesus told the apostles, "Whatever you bind on earth shall be bound in heaven, and whatever you loose on earth shall be loosed in heaven" (Matt. 18:18). He also told them to treat those who don't submit to the judgment of Church leaders as a "Gentile or tax collector"—that's to say, an outcast (Matt. 18:15-17).

Baptism, therefore, imposes upon us the obligation to always have a reverential deference to the judgment of Holy Mother Church. And in those matters when the Church binds us to believe something that has to do with faith and morals, we must assent definitively and wholeheartedly. God help us, that we may be faithful sons and daughters of Holy Mother Church.

Conclusion

Like the folks present in Jerusalem on the day of Pentecost, many to whom we proclaim the gospel message will ask, "What shall we do?"—the implication being what they must do *to be saved*. With St. Peter, we can proclaim with full confidence, "Repent, and be baptized every one of you in the name of Jesus Christ for the forgiveness of your sins; and you shall receive the gift of the Holy Spirit" (Acts 2:28).

You could say that this book has been our way of unpacking Peter's answer, providing the evidence and catechesis surrounding the claim that baptism saves. With Christ, we desire all to be "born again" by water and Spirit and become sons and daughters of God the Father in the new covenantal family of God, the Church. And with such new life, God's children have access to all the gifts Christ invested his Church with—the sacraments, along with the Church's liturgical worship. Just as God wills us to be birthed into a familial life on the natural level, he wills all to be birthed into a familial life on the supernatural level, which is the life of the Church.

Baptism, therefore, is just as much communal as it is personal. It saves us on the individual level. But it also saves us in and *through* the Church, the body of Christ (Col. 1:24).

May God give us the grace to be faithful to what this new circumcision of Christ entails all the way until death, and may we receive our inheritance as sons and daughters of the Father by finally entering the everlasting kingdom of heaven prepared for us.

About the Author

Karlo Broussard, DPhil., a native of Southern Louisiana, left a promising musical career to devote himself full-time to the work of Catholic apologetics. As a staff apologist and speaker for Catholic Answers, and a member of the chancery evangelization team at the Diocese of Tulsa and Eastern Oklahoma, he travels the country and the diocese giving talks on apologetics, biblical studies, theology, and philosophy. Karlo is a regular guest on *Catholic Answers Live* and contributor to *Catholic Answers Magazine*.

Karlo holds a doctorate in philosophy from the Pontifical University St. Patrick's in Maynooth, Ireland, as well as undergraduate and graduate degrees in theology from Catholic Distance University and the Augustine Institute, and a master's in philosophy from Holy Apostles College and Seminary.

A dynamic and gifted Catholic speaker and author, Karlo is known for communicating with precision of thought, a genuine love for God, and an enthusiasm that inspires.

Endnotes

1 There are two things to note here about the emphases in this statement. First, I emphasize *merely* because, as we will see, the Catholic Church affirms that there is a symbolic value to the sacrament of baptism. It wouldn't be a sacrament without such symbolism. Second, I emphasize *salvation* to distinguish one kind of mere symbolism—namely, baptism is merely a symbol of *salvation*, from the belief that baptism is merely a symbol of God's grace working in your heart. The reason for this is that some Christians affirm that baptism gives grace—a grace that increases our sanctity after the initial grace of salvation has been given—but deny that baptism gives the initial grace of *salvation*, professing that baptism merely symbolizes it. Protestant apologist Gavin Ortlund articulates this view as his own. In his online video entitled "Baptismal Regeneration: Responding to Common Arguments," he states, "So if we were to take a distinction here between the grace by which God brings us into a state of salvation and the grace by which God nourishes and strengthens and furthers us in our salvation, the Baptist tradition puts baptism in the latter category. It's not the cause." See Gavin Ortlund, "Baptismal Regeneration: Responding to Common Arguments," YouTube video, https://www.youtube.com/watch?v=C4BoIc2-P8M&t=0s. Ortlund later states in the same video concerning this relation between baptism and salvation: "No, I don't think that's actually what happens when you're baptized, I don't think baptism causes that. I think it's associated with that, it symbolizes that, it seals

that and so forth, but it's not actually the cause of that." My interest in this book is not whether baptism is merely a symbol of grace. Rather, my interest is whether baptism merely is a symbol of *salvation*.

2 Council of Trent, Session VII, *Decree Concerning the Sacraments*, "Touching on Baptism," can. 2, 3 March, 1547, in *The Canons and Decrees on the Council of Trent*, trans. Theodore A. Buckley (New York, NY: George Routledge and Co., 1851), 53.

3 Kaufmann Kohler and Samuel Kraus, "Baptism," *Jewish Encyclopedia*, www.jewishencyclopedia.com.

4 George R. Beasley-Murray, *John*, vol. 36, *Word Biblical Commentary* (Dallas: Word, Incorporated, 2002), 49.

5 Todd Baker, *Exodus from Rome: A Biblical and Historical Critique of Roman Catholicism* (Bloomington, IN: iUniverse, 2014), ch. 11; Kindle Edition. Emphasis added.

6 See ibid.

7 See ibid.

8 Ron Rhodes, *Reasoning from the Scriptures with Catholics* (Eugene, OR: Harvest House Publishers, 2000), 166.

9 See *The Ignatius Catholic Study Bible: The New Testament* (San Francisco: Ignatius Press, 2010), 166.

10 Stanley Fowler, *Rethinking Baptism: Some Baptist Reflections* (Eugene, OR: Wipf and Stock, 2015), 27.

11 D.A. Carson, *The Gospel According to John*, The Pillar New Testament Commentary (Grand Rapids, MI: Eerdmans Publishing, 1991), 191.

12 Leadership Ministries Worldwide, *The Preacher's Outline & Sermon Bible: John (The Preacher's Outline & Sermon Bible KJV)* (Chattanooga, TN: Leadership Ministries Worldwide, 2017), 53.

13 Baker, *Exodus from Rome*, ch. 11.

14 Ibid.

15 Ibid.

16 *The Preacher's Outline & Sermon Bible*, 53.

17 Baker, *Exodus from Rome*, ch. 11, emphasis added.

18 Ibid.

19 *Catechism of the Catholic Church*, 2nd ed. (Rome: Libreria Editrice Vaticana, 1994).

20 B.M. Newman Jr., *A Concise Greek-English Dictionary of the New Testament*, 46. See also *A Greek-English Lexicon of the New Testament and Other Early Christian Literature*, 3rd ed. eds., William F. Arndt, F. Wilbur Gingrich, and F.W. Danker (Chicago: University of Chicago Press, 2000), 249.

21 More work would need to be done to show that interior righteousness is the *sole* formal cause of our justification as the Council of Trent teaches: "[T]he sole formal cause is the justice of God; not that by which He himself is just, but that by which He maketh us just, that, to wit, with which *we*, being endowed by Him, are renewed in the spirit of our mind." Council of Trent, Session VI, *Decree Concerning Justification*, ch. 7, 13 January, 1547, in *The Canons and Decrees on the Council of Trent*, 34.

22 Baker, *Exodus from Rome*, Vol. I, ch. 11.

23 Douglas J. Moo, *The Epistle to the Romans*, New International Commentary on the New Testament (Grand Rapids, MI: Eerdmans, 1996), 359.

24 Baker, *Exodus from Rome*, Vol. 1, ch. 11. Baker is not the only one who makes this argument. As a reference, he cites James W. Dale, *Christic Baptism and Patristic Baptism* (Phillipsburg, NJ: P&R Publishing, 1995), 242.

25 See Norman L. Geisler and Ralph E. MacKenzie, *Roman Catholics and Evangelicals: Agreements and Differences* (Ada, MI: Baker Academic, 1995), 481-482.

26 For other examples where Jesus uses the "not . . . but" formula for hyperbolic speech, see Matthew 10:20; John 6:27, 12:44.

27 See Rhodes, *Reasoning from the Scriptures with Catholics*, 163-164.

28 I am grateful to Jimmy Akin for this line of reasoning.

29 See Rhodes, *Reasoning from the Scriptures*, 163-164. See also Geisler and MacKenzie, *Roman Catholics and Evangelicals*, 480-483, 488-489; Ortlund, "Baptismal Regeneration."

30 See Craig Keener, "Holy Spirit," *The Lexham Bible Dictionary*, ed. John D. Barry et al. (Bellingham, WA: Lexham Press, 2016).

31 See Keener, "Holy Spirit," *The Lexham Bible Dictionary*.

32 Everett Ferguson, *Baptism in the Early Church: History, Theology, and Liturgy in the First Five Centuries* (Grand Rapids, MI: Eerdmans, 2013), 177, emphasis added. I am grateful to Trent Horn for this research. See Trent Horn, "REBUTTING Gavin Ortlund on baptismal regeneration," YouTube video, https://www.youtube.com/watch?v=4cp5ZWCDneo.

33 See Thomas Aquinas, *Summa Theologiae* III:69:4 ad 2.

34 This line of argumentation was taken from C.S. Dessain, "The Acts of the Apostles," in *A Catholic Commentary on Holy Scripture*, eds. B. Orchard and E.F. Sutcliffe (New York: Thomas Nelson, 1953), 1022.

35 Seek Baker, *Exodus from Rome*, Vol. I, ch. 11. Gavin Ortlund makes this same argument in his discussion with Trent Horn on baptismal regeneration. See Gavin Ortlund and Trent Horn, "Trent Horn and Gavin Ortlund on Baptism," YouTube Video, https://www.youtube.com/watch?v=JGwECD_Dv3k.

36 Baker, *Exodus from Rome*, ch. 11.

37 Other passages that Baker cites are Acts 10:47–48; 16:14–15, 31–33; 18:8; 19:4–5.

38 See Aquinas, *Summa Theologiae* I-II:113:4; III:85:6; II-II:6:2.

39 See ibid., II-II:2:1.

40 See Ortlund "Baptismal Regeneration"; Ortlund and Horn, "On Baptism."

41 See Horn, "REBUTTING Gavin Ortlund on baptismal regeneration."

42 Baker, *Exodus from Rome*, ch. 11.

43 *A Greek-English Lexicon of the New Testament and Other Early Christian Literature*, 362. See also B.M. Newman Jr., *A Concise Greek-English Dictionary of the New Testament* (Deutsche Bibelgesellschaft: United Bible Societies, 1993), 67.

44 "A formal request, *appeal.*" *A Greek-English Lexicon of the New Testament and Other Early Christian Literature*, 362. "That which is asked for—'request, appeal.'" J.P. Louw and E.A. Nida, *Greek-English Lexicon of the New Testament: Based on Semantic Domains* (Deutsche Bibelgesellschaft: United Bible Societies, 1996), 406.

45 Baker, *Exodus from Rome*, ch. 11.

46 B.M. Newman Jr., *A Concise Greek-English Dictionary of the New Testament*, 46. See also *A Greek-English Lexicon of the New Testament and Other Early Christian Literature*, 249.

47 Baker makes this argument as well in his *Exodus from Rome*, ch. 11.

48 Ortlund, "Baptismal Regeneration."

49 See Baker, *Exodus from Rome*, ch. 11.

50 Ibid.

51 Ibid. Emphasis added.

52 M.S. Heiser and V.M. Setterholm, *Glossary of Morpho-Syntactic Database Terminology* (Bellingham, WA: Lexham Press, 2013), "aorist" entry.

53 Ignatius of Antioch, *The Epistle to the Trallians*, in *The Apostolic Fathers with Justin Martyr and Irenaeus: Volume I*, eds. A. Roberts, J. Donaldson and A. C. Coxe (Fort Washington, PA: Christian Literature Company, 1885), 67-81.

54 Ignatius of Antioch, *The Epistle to the Philippians* in *The Apostolic Fathers with Justin Martyr and Irenaeus: Volume I*, eds. A. Roberts, J. Donaldson and A. C. Coxe (Fort Washington, PA: Christian Literature Company, 1885), 116.

55 Scholars acknowledge that this letter was not written by the apostle Barnabas mentioned in the New Testament. Rather, it's attributed to an otherwise early Christian teacher who is unknown to us.

56 Some date *The Shepherd* to no later than A.D. 145 because The Muratorian Fragment states that Hermas wrote *The Shepherd* while his brother, Pope Pius I, was still alive. It states, "But Hermas wrote The Shepherd 'most recently in our time,' in the city of Rome, while bishop Pius, his brother, was occupying the chair of the church of the city of Rome." Others, however, date *The Shepherd* to around A.D. 80. See Jimmy Akin, *The Fathers Know Best: Your Essential Guide to the Teachings of the Early Church* (El Cajon, CA: Catholic Answers, 2010), ch. 3. One reason for this early dating is that it mentions a man named "Clement," who most think is Clement of Rome, the author of the first-century Letter to the Corinthians. Here's the relevant quote (bk. 2, vision 2, ch. 4), according to the translation of J.B. Lightfoot: "Thou shalt therefore write two little books, and shalt send one to Clement, and one to Grapte. So Clement shall send to the foreign cities, for this is his duty; while Grapte shall instruct the widows and the orphans." *The Shepherd* 2:2:4, trans. J.B. Lightfoot, https://www.earlychristianwritings.com/

text/shepherd-lightfoot.html#google_vignette. If this is Clement of Rome from the first century, the author of the Letter to the Corinthians, then *The Shepherd* was written in the first century, anywhere from A.D. 70 to 97. The reason for this date range is that Clement of Rome was probably a secretary of sorts in the church of Rome around A.D. 70 and, according to the historical record, was bishop of Rome from A.D. 88 to 97.

57 The Shepherd of Hermas, 2:4:3, in *Fathers of the Second Century: Hermas, Tatian, Athenagoras, Theophilus, and Clement of Alexandria (Entire)*, vol. 2, eds. A. Roberts, J. Donaldson, and A. Coxe, trans. F. Crombie (Buffalo, NY: Christian Literature Company, 1885), 22.

58 Ibid., 3:9:16, pg. 49.

59 St. Justin Martyr, *First Apology*, ch. 61, in *The Apostolic Fathers with Justin Martyr and Irenaeus*, vol. 1, eds. A. Roberts, J. Donaldson, and A. C. Coxe (Buffalo, NY: Christian Literature Company, 1885), 183, emphasis added.

60 Ibid.

61 Ibid., emphasis added.

62 Ortlund, "Baptismal Regeneration."

63 St. Justin Martyr, *Dialogue with Trypho the Jew*, ch. 14, in *The Apostolic Fathers with Justin Martyr and Irenaeus*, 201, emphasis added.

64 Ortlund, "Baptismal Regeneration," emphasis added.

65 St. Irenaeus, *Against Heresies*, 3:17, in *The Apostolic Fathers with Justin Martyr and Irenaeus*, vol. 1, eds. A. Roberts, J. Donaldson, & A. C. Coxe (Buffalo, NY: Christian Literature Company, 1885), 444. Irenaeus teaches the same thing later in book five, chapter fifteen of the same work.

66 Ibid.

67 Ibid., emphasis added.

68 St. Irenaeus, *On the Apostolic Preaching*, §3, trans. John Behr (Crestwood, NY: St. Vladimir's Seminary Press, 1997), 42, emphasis added.

69 Ibid., §41, emphasis added.

70 St. Clement of Alexandria, *The Instructor*, 1:6, in *Fathers of the Second Century: Hermas, Tatian, Athenagoras, Theophilus, and Clement of Alexandria (Entire)*, vol. 2, eds. A. Roberts, J. Donaldson, and A. C. Coxe (Buffalo, NY: Christian Literature Company, 1885), 215-217, emphasis added.

71 Tertullian, *On Baptism* 12:1, in *Latin Christianity: Its Founder, Tertullian*, vol. 3, trans. S. Thelwall, eds. A. Roberts, J. Donaldson, & A. C. Coxe (Buffalo, NY: Christian Literature Company, 1885), 674-675, emphasis added.

72 St. Hippolytus, *Discourse on the Holy Theophany* 8, emphasis added.

73 St. Athanasius, *On the Incarnation of the Word*, 54.3, in *St. Athanasius: Select Works and Letters*, vol. 4, trans. A.T. Robertson, eds. P. Schaff and H. Wace (Buffalo, NY: Christian Literature Company, 1892), 65.

74 St. John Chrysostom, *Baptismal Catecheses in Augustine, Against Julian* 1:6:21, emphasis added.

75 St. Cyril of Jerusalem, *Catechetical Lectures* 3.10, in *S. Cyril of Jerusalem, S. Gregory Nazianzen*, Vol. 7, trans. R.W. Church and E.H. Gifford, eds. P. Schaff and H. Wace (Buffalo, NY: Christian Literature Company, 1894), 16, emphasis added.

76 Ibid., 17, emphasis added.

77 Cyril, *Catechetical Lectures* 3.4, in *S. Cyril of Jerusalem, S. Gregory Nazianzen*, 15, emphasis added.

78 Ortlund, "Baptismal Regeneration."

79 Ibid.

80 Council of Trent, *Decree on Justification*, ch. 7, in *The Canons and Decrees of the Council of Trent*, 33-34.

81 Cyril, *Catechetical Lectures* 3.4.

82 J.N.D. Kelly, *Early Christian Doctrines*, 5th ed. (New York, NY: Continuum, 1977), 193-94, emphasis added.

83 William Webster, *The Church of Rome at the Bar of History* (Carlisle, PA: Banner of Truth, 1997), 95.

84 Pope Leo XIII, Encyclical Letter on the Study of Sacred Scripture *Providentisimus Deus* §14, November 18, 1893, https://www.vatican.va/content/leo-xiii/en/encyclicals/documents/hf_l-xiii_enc_18111893_providentissimus-deus.html, emphasis added.

85 Apologist Jimmy Akin affirms that such terminology indicates that something is "an infallibly defined teaching." See Jimmy Akin, "The 'Unanimous Consent' of the Church Fathers," *National Catholic Register*, August 18, 2018, https://www.ncregister.com/blog/the-unanimous-consent-of-the-church-fathers. That such an infallibly defined teaching is *part of divine revelation* is inferred from the language used by the Congregation for the Doctrine of the Faith in its "Doctrinal Commentary on concluding formula of 'Professio fidei,'" where it speaks of those teachings that are part of divine revelation as being "divine and Catholic faith." See also Congregation for the Doctrine of the Faith, "Doctrinal Commentary on concluding formula of 'Professio fidei,'" June 29, 1998, https://www.ewtn.com/catholicism/library/doctrinal-commentary-on-concluding-formula-of-professio-fidei-2038.

86 There is ambiguity as to whether this is the fifteenth or sixteenth council of Carthage. See Heinrich Denzinger,

Enchiridion Symbolorum Definitionum et Declarationum De Rebus Fidei et Morum: Compendium of Creeds, Definitions, and Declarations on Matters of Faith and Morals, eds. Peter Hünermann, Robert Fastiggi, and Anne Englund Nash, 43rd edition (San Francisco: Ignatius, 2012), 82.

87 Fifteenth Council of Carthage, "Original Sin," can. 2, in Denzinger, *Enchiridion Symbolorum*, 82, DH 223, emphasis added.

88 Originally, these teachings were attributed to Pope Celestine I. But subsequent scholarship has shown this to be false. However, they are recognized to be a collection of decrees from the See of Rome that were, around the year 500, included in a collection of decrees by Dionysius Exiguus entitled *Decretalium Collectioni* (Collection of Decretals). See Denzinger, *Enchiridion Symbolorum*, 88.

89 See ibid.

90 *Doctrinal Judgments of the Former Bishops of the Apostolic See on the Grace of God and the Free Choice of the Will*, ch. 1, in Denzinger, *Enchiridion Symbolorum*, 88, DH 239, emphasis added.

91 Second Council of Orange, can. 5, in Denzinger, *Enchiridion Symbolorum*, 135, DH 375, emphasis added.

92 Third Council of Valence, *On Predestination*, can. 5, in Denzinger, *Enchiridion Symbolorum*, 217, DH 632, emphasis added.

93 Council of Vienne, Constitution *Fidei Catholicae*, in Denzinger, *Enchiridion Symbolorum*, 290, DH 903, emphasis added.

94 Ibid., 291, DH 904, emphasis added.

95 Pope Eugene IV, Bull of Union with the Armenians *Exsultate Deo* (November 22, 1439), in Denzinger, *Enchiridion Symbolorum*, 338-339, DH 1312-1313, emphasis added.

96 Council of Trent, Session V, *The Decree on Original Sin*, 17 June, 1546, in *The Canons and Decrees of the Council of Trent*, 23, emphasis added.

97 Council of Trent, *The Decree on Justification*, ch. 4, in *The Canons and Decrees of the Council of Trent*, 31-32, emphasis added.

98 Ibid., 33-34, emphasis added.

99 Council of Trent, *Decree Concerning the Sacraments*, "Touching on Baptism," can. 5, in *The Canons and Decrees of the Council of Trent*, 53, emphasis added.

100 Irenaeus, *A Discourse in Demonstration of the Apostolic Preaching* 3.

101 Fourth Lateran Council, *The Catholic Faith*, in Heinrich Denzinger, *Enchiridion Symbolorum Definitionum et Declarationum De Rebus Fidei et Morum: Compendium of Creeds, Definitions, and Declarations on Matters of Faith and Morals*, eds. Peter Hünermann, Robert Fastiggi, and Anne Englund Nash, 43rd edition (San Francisco: Ignatius, 2012), 267, DH 802.

102 Pope Eugene IV, Bull of Union with the Armenians *Exsultate Deo* (November 22, 1439), DH 1316, emphasis added.

103 See Aquinas, *Summa Theologiae* III:67:3.

104 Ibid., trans. Fathers of the English Dominican Province (Cincinnati, OH: Benziger Brothers, 1947).

105 Ibid.

106 Ibid.

107 Tertullian, *On Baptism*, ch. 17, in *Latin Christianity*, 677.

108 See ibid. "For how credible would it seem, that he who has not permitted a woman even to learn with over-boldness, should give a female the power of teaching and of baptizing!"

109 "If someone is traveling by sea in a foreign place or if there is no church in the vicinity, a believer who has kept his baptism intact and is not a bigamist may baptize a catechumen if there is an exigency of sickness, on condition that, if (the catechumen) survives, he will bring him to the bishop, so that he might be perfected by the imposition of hands." Council of Elvira, can. 38, DH 120.

110 "If necessity so be, we know that even laymen may, and frequently do, baptize. For as a man receives, so too he can give." Jerome, *The Dialogue Against the Luciferians*, in *St. Jerome: Letters and Select Works*, Vol. 6, trans. W.H. Remantle, G. Lewis, and W.G. Martley, eds. P. Schaff and H. Wace (Christian Literature Company, 1893), 324.

111 See Augustine, *Contra Epistulam Parmeniani Libri Tres*, II, 13, 29.

112 See Pope Urban II, *Epistle* 271.

113 See Ludwig Ott, *The Fundamentals of Catholic Dogma* (St. Louis, Missouri: B. Herder Book Company, 1957), 358.

114 "You say that in your country many [have been] baptized by a certain Jew (you do not know whether he is Christian or pagan), and you are asking what should be done about them. If they were truly baptized in the name of the Holy Trinity or only in the name of Christ, as we read in the Acts of the Apostles [2:38; 19:5] (for it is one an the same thing, as St. Ambrose explains), it is clear that they should not be baptized again." Pope Nicholas I, "From the responses to the decrees of the Bulgars," November 866, DH 646.

115 See Cyprian, Epistle 73 (74), "To Pompey, Against the Epistle to Stephen About the Baptism of Heretics," in *The Ante-Nicene Fathers*, vol. 5, *Fathers of the Third Century: Hippolytus, Cyprian, Novatian, Appendix*, trans. R.E. Wallis, eds. A. Roberts, J. Donaldson, and A.C. Coxe (Christian Literature Company, 1886), 386.

116 "If any come to you from any heresy whatever, let nothing be introduced except what is already handed down, [namely,] that a hand be imposed on them for penance one who comes to them from another group but simply admit him to their communion." Pope Stephen I, "Fragment of a Letter to Cyprian," from Cyprian *Epistle* 73 (74), DH 110.

117 Council of Trent, *Decree Concerning the Sacraments*, "Touching on Baptism," can. 4, in *The Canons and Decrees of the Council of Trent*, 53.

118 Aquinas, *Summa Theologiae* III:68:10.

119 Ibid.

120 I am grateful to Joe Heschmeyer for this line of reasoning. See Joe Heschmeyer, "Can I Secretly Baptize My Grandchildren?", Catholic Answers, November 7, 2023, https://www.catholic.com/magazine/online-edition/can-i-secretly-baptize-my-grandchildren.

121 See Aquinas, *Summa Theologiae* III:68:10 ad 1.

122 Ibid., ad 3.

123 See Cyprian, *Epistle* 73 (74), "Against the Epistle to Stephen About the Baptism of Heretics."

124 See Pope Stephen I, "Fragment of a Letter to Cyprian." See also Stephen I, "Fragment of a Letter to Cyprian," from Firmilianus's Letter to Cyprian Against the Letter of Stephen," DH 111: "[Stephen says] But in many ways the name of Christ contributes . . . to the faith and the sanctification of baptism, so that whoever in any place has been baptized in the name of Christ receives at once the grace of Christ."

125 See Pope St. Gregory II, Letter to St. Boniface "Desiderabilem Mihi," November 22, 726, DH 580: "Whoever has been baptized in the name of the Father and of the Son and of the Holy Spirit may in no case be rebaptized; for not in the name

of the one baptizing, but in the name of the Trinity has one received the gift of this gracer. And let that which the apostle says be observed: One God, one faith, one baptism [cf. Eph. 4:5]."

126 See Council of Lyon II, "Profession of Faith of Michael Palaeologus," DH 855: "Because of various errors, introduced by some through ignorance and by others out of malice, she [the Church] says and preaches: Those who after baptism lapse into sin must not be rebaptized but must obtain pardon for their sins through true penance." See also Council of Trent, *Decree Concerning the Sacraments*, "Touching on Baptism," can. 11, in *The Canons and Decrees of the Council of Trent*, 54: "If anyone shall say, that baptism, true, and rightly conferred, is to be repeated for him who, amongst Infidels, has denied the faith of Christ, when he is converted unto penitence; let him be anathema."

127 Council of Trent, *Decree Concerning the Sacraments*, "Touching on Baptism," can. 13, in *The Canons and Decrees of the Council of Trent*, 54.

128 Aquinas, *Summa Theologiae* III:68:11.

129 See ibid., art. 7 resp.

130 Taken from Aquinas, *Summa Theologiae* III:68:4.

131 Ibid.

132 Ibid.

133 Canon 4 of the Council of Hippo reads thus: "Care must be taken also that the weakness of the brothers shall not believe that it is possible to baptize the dead, when he notices that the Eucharist is not being given to the dead." Council of Hippo, trans. Roger Pearse in "Canons 1-4 of the breviarium of the Council of Hippo (393)," https://www.roger-pearse.com/weblog/2021/04/01/canons-1-4-of-the-breviarium-of-the-council-of-hippo-393. Canon 18

of the Council of Carthage reads as follows: "Neither the Eucharist nor baptism should be given to the bodies of the dead." Council of Carthage, https://www.newadvent.org/fathers/3816.htm.

134 The Church of Jesus Christ of Latter-day Saints, "Baptisms for the Dead," churchofjesuschrist.org.

135 See Ludwig Ott, *Fundamentals of Catholic Dogma*, 359.

136 See Curtis Mitch and Scott Hahn, *The Ignatius Catholic Study Bible: The New Testament* (San Francisco, CA: Ignatius Press, 2010), 307.

137 See "Brephos," in *A Greek-English Lexicon of the New Testament and Other Early Christian Literature*, 183.

138 I am grateful to Jimmy Akin for this line of argumentation. See Jimmy Akin, *A Daily Defense: 365 Days (Plus One) to Becoming a Better Apologist* (El Cajon, CA: Catholic Answers Press, 2016), 75.

139 *The Greek New Testament: SBL Edition*, ed. Michael W. Holmes (Logos Bible Software), Electronic edition.

140 Martin Luther, *The Babylonian Captivity of the Church 1520: The Annotated Luther Study Edition*, ed. Paul W. Robinson (Minneapolis: Fortress Press, 2016), 100.

141 Baker, *Exodus from Rome*, Vol. 1, ch. 11.

142 Ibid.

143 I am grateful to Tim Staples for this line of argumentation. See Tim Staples, "Where Is Infant Baptism in the Bible?", Catholic Answers, January 2, 2025, https://www.catholic.com/magazine/online-edition/infant-baptism.

144 *A Greek-English Lexicon of the New Testament*, 1007.

145 See ibid.

146 Council of Trent, *Decree on Original Sin*, in *The Canons and Decrees of the Council of Trent*, 22.

147 St. Thomas Aquinas makes this argument in his *Summa Theologiae* III:68:9. The Council of Trent follows suit and roots its teaching on infant baptism in the reality of original sin: "by reason of this rule of faith, from a tradition of the apostles, even infants, who could not as yet in themselves commit any sin, are for this cause truly *baptized for the remission of sins*, that in them that which they have contracted by generation, may be cleansed away by regeneration." Council of Trent, *Decree on Original Sin*, in *The Canons and Decrees*, 23. The *Catechism of the Catholic Church* reaffirms this line of argumentation in paragraph 403.

148 Irenaeus, *Against Heresies* 2:22:4, in *The Apostolic Fathers*, 391.

149 *Fragments from the Lost Writings of Irenaeus* 34, in *The Apostolic Fathers*, 574, emphasis added.

150 Hippolytus, *The Apostolic Tradition* 21:4, trans. Burton Scott Easton (New Haven, CT: Archon Books, 1962), available online at https://www.gutenberg.org/files/61614/61614-h/61614-h.htm, emphasis added.

151 Origen, *Commentary on the Epistle to the Romans* 5.9, trans. Thomas P. Scheck (Washington D.C.: Catholic University of America Press, 2001), 367, emphasis added.

152 Origin, *Homilies on Leviticus* 8:3:11, trans. Gary Wayne Barkley, ed. Gary Wayne Barkley (Washington, D.C.: Catholic University of America Press, 2010), 158, emphasis added.

153 Ibid.

154 Cyprian, *Letters* 58:2, in *Fathers of the Third Century*, 353-354.

155 See Geisler and MacKenzie, *Roman Catholics and Evangelicals*, 481.

156 Aquinas, *Summa Theologiae* III:68:9.

157 This line of argumentation was taken from "Infant Baptism," Catholic Answers, https://www.catholic.com/tract/infant-baptism.

158 Gavin Ortlund, "DIALOGUE: Answering Gavin Ortlund's baptism questions," YouTube Video, https://www.youtube.com/watch?v=jxDaUGNIdBM.

159 See Baker, *Exodus from Rome*, Vol. I, ch. 11.

160 See Jacque Lafleur, *The Science of Salvation: Forty-Nine Instant Sermons Especially for Lay Pastors* (Fort Oglethorpe, GA: TEACH Services, Inc., 2009), 213; First Baptist Independence, "Baptism," http://www.fbionline.org/connect/baptism.

161 See First Baptist Independence, "Baptism."

162 Bernard Drachman and Kaufmann Kohler, "Ablution," *Jewish Encyclopedia*, www.jewishencyclopedia.com.

163 See Tim Staples, "Dunk, Pour, or Sprinkle? How to Baptize New Testament Style," Catholic Answers, May 17, 2017, https://www.catholic.com/magazine/online-edition/dunk-pour-or-sprinkle-how-to-baptize-new-testament-style.

164 Kohler and Kraus, "Baptism."

165 Catholic Answers, "Baptism: Immersion Only?", https://www.catholic.com/tract/baptism-immersion-only.

166 This line of argumentation is taken from ibid.

167 *The Didache*, ch. 7, in *The Ante-Nicene Fathers*, Vol. 7, *Fathers of the Third and Fourth Centuries: Lactantius, Venantius, Asterius, Victorinus, Dionysius, Apostolic Teaching and Constitutions, Homily, and Liturgies*, eds., A. Roberts, J. Donaldson, and A.C. Coxe, (Fort Washington, PA: Christian Literature Company, 1886), 379.

168 Hippolytus, *The Apostolic Tradition* 21.

169 Pope Cornelius, *Letter to Fabius of Antioch*, http://prenicea.net/doc3/31601-en-01.pdf.

170 Cyprian, *Letter 75*, in *The Ante-Nicene Fathers*, Vol. 5, *Fathers of the Third Century*, 400.

171 Pope Eugene IV, Bull of Union with the Armenians *Exsultate Deo*, in Denzinger, *Enchiridion Symbolorum*, 339, DH 1314, emphasis added.

172 Council of Trent, *Decree on the Sacraments*, "Touching on Baptism," can. 4, in *The Canons and Decrees of the Council of Trent*, 53.

173 *Didache*, ch. 7, in *Fathers of the Third and Fourth Centuries*, 379, emphasis added.

174 St. Justin Martyr, *First Apology*, ch. 61, in *The Apostolic Fathers with Justin Martyr and Irenaeus*, 183, emphasis added.

175 St. Irenaeus, *On the Apostolic Preaching*, §3, 42, emphasis added.

176 Hippolytus, *The Apostolic Tradition* 21:12-18, emphasis added.

177 Tertullian, *Against Praxeas* 26, in *Latin Christianity*, 623, emphasis added.

178 Origen, *Commentary on the Epistle to the Romans* 5.8, 356, emphasis added.

179 Cyprian of Carthage, *Letters* 73:18, *Fathers of the Third Century*, 383, emphasis added.

180 Eusebius of Caesarea, *Letter to the People of His Diocese* 3, trans. taken from New Advent.org, https://www.newadvent.org/fathers/2804.htm, emphasis added.

181 Pope Nicholas I, Responses *Ad consulta vestra* to the Bulgarians, ch. 104, November 13, 866, in Denzinger, *Enchiridion Symbolorum*, 221-222, DH 646, emphasis added.

182 Pope Pelagius I, Letter *Admonemus ut* to Bishop Gaudentius of Volterra, between September 558 and February 2, 559, in Denzinger, *Enchiridion Symbolorum*, 156, DH 445, emphasis added.

183 Congregation for the Doctrine of the Faith, "New Response of the Congregation for the Doctrine of the Faith on the Validity of Baptism, March 9, 2012, https://www.vatican.va/roman_curia/congregations/cfaith/documents/rc_con_cfaith_doc_20080201_validity-baptism-miralles_en.html, emphasis added.

184 Ibid.

185 Ibid., emphasis added.

186 Aquinas, *Summa Theologiae* III:68:5. Cf. III:69:2.

187 Council of Trent, *Decree on the Sacraments*, "Touching on the Sacraments in General," can. 4, in *The Canons and Decrees of the Council of Trent*, 52.

188 See YouTube video, "CALive | Baptism, Salvation, and More with Karlo Broussard | August 7th, 2023," time code: 1:16:17, https://www.youtube.com/watch?v=Z6q8vQ0-WeU.

189 See Aquinas, *Summa Theologiae* III:68:3.

190 Council of Trent, *Decree on Justification*, ch. 4, in *The Canons and Decrees of the Council of Trent*, 31–32, emphasis added.

191 St. Ambrose, *Consolation on the Death of Valentinian* 51, 53, quoted in Ott, *The Fundamentals of Catholic Dogma*, 357.

192 St. Augustine, *On Baptism* 4.22.29, quoted in Ott, *The Fundamentals of Catholic Dogma*, 357.

193 For a list of these figures and their works, see Ott, *The Fundamentals of Catholic Dogma*, 357.

194 This letter was attributed by some to Pope Innocent III. But it is now known to be written by Pope Innocent II during his

reign as pope (1130-1143). See Denzinger, *Enchiridion Symbolorum*, 243, DH 741.

195 Pope Innocent II, Letter *Apostolicam Sedem* (Apostolic See) to the Bishop of Cremona, date uncertain, in Denzinger, *Enchiridion Symbolorum*, 243, DH 741, emphasis added.

196 Pope Innocent III, Letter *Debitum Officii Pontificalis* to Bishop Berthold of Metz, August 28, 1206, in Denzinger, *Enchiridion Symbolorum*, 261, DH 788, emphasis added.

197 Pope Pius IX, *On Promotion of False Doctrines*, sec. 7, 1863, https://www.papalencyclicals.net/pius09/p9quanto.htm, emphasis added.

198 Pope Pius XII, Encyclical Letter *Mystici Corporis Christi*, sec. 103, June 29, 1943, https://www.vatican.va/content/pius-xii/en/encyclicals/documents/hf_p-xii_enc_29061943_mystici-corporis-christi.html, emphasis added.

199 It's interesting to note that Aquinas went so far as to say that God, in his providence, would see to it that a person would have an opportunity to make an explicit act of faith before death, either because God "would reveal to him through internal inspiration what had to be believed [which would include the truth about the necessity of baptism for salvation] or would send some preacher of the faith to him as he sent Peter to Cornelius [Acts 10:20]." Aquinas, *De Veritate* 14:11 ad 1, trans. James V. McGlynn (Chicago: Henry Regnery Company, 1953), https://isidore.co/aquinas/QDdeVer14.htm.

200 The Church has taught with a very high degree of authority (perhaps even infallibly in the minds of some) that *if* anyone dies with original sin only, then such a soul wouldn't be able to enter the beatific vision. Consider, for example, Pope Eugene IV's papal bull *Laetentur Caeli* issued at the Council of Florence. It states, "Likewise, [we define] . . . the souls of those who die

in actual moral sin or with original sin only, they go down immediately to hell, to be punished, however, with different punishments." Pope Eugene IV, *Laetentur Caeli*, July 6, 1439, in Denzinger, *Enchiridion Symbolorum*, 336, DH 1306. As to *whether* an individual, like an infant, *in fact* dies in such a state, we don't know. This is why the Church permits a diversity of theological opinions.

201 See International Theological Commission, *The Hope of Salvation for Infants Who Die Without Being Baptized*, January 19, 2007, https://www.vatican.va/roman_curia/congregations/cfaith/cti_documents/rc_con_cfaith_doc_20070419_un-baptised-infants_en.html#:~:text=The%20International%20Theological%20Commission%20has,of%20Christ%2C%20the%20sacramentality%20of, footnote #52.

202 "The doctrine that rejects as a Pelagian fable that place in the netherworld (which the faithful commonly designate by the name of the limbo of children) in which the soul of the dead with only original sin are punished with the punishment of damnation without the punishment of fire, as if those who remove the punishment of fire were thereby introducing some intermediate place and state exempt from guilt and punishment between the kingdom of God and eternal damnation, as the Pelagians have imagined, [is] false, rash, and injurious to Catholic schools." Pope Pius VI, Papal Bull *Auctorem Fidei*, Proposition 26, 1794, in Denzinger, *Enchiridion Symbolorum*, pg. 535–536, DH 2626.

203 International Theological Commission, *The Hope of Salvation for Infants*, sec. 40.

204 Trent Horn and Gavin Ortlund, "DIALOGUE: Answering Gavin Ortlund's Baptism Questions," YouTube Video, https://www.youtube.com/watch?v=jxDaUGNIdBM.

205 See Gavin Ortlund, "Baptismal Regeneration: Responding to Common Arguments," YouTube video, https://www.youtube.com/watch?v=C4BoIc2-P8M&t=0s.

206 See Council of Trent, *Decree on Justification*, ch. 8.

207 See J. Pohle, J. and A. Preuss, *The Sacraments: A Dogmatic Treatise*, Vol. 1 (St. Louis, MO; London: B. Herder, 1917), 128.

208 Council of Trent, *Decree on Justification*, ch. 7, in *The Canons and Decrees of the Council of Trent*, 34.

209 Ibid.

210 See Aquinas, *Summa Theologiae* III:68:8.

211 See ibid., II-II:6:2.

212 See Pohle and Preuss, *The Sacraments*, 128.

213 Council of Trent, *Decree on Justification*, ch. 6, in *The Canons and Decrees of the Council of Trent*, 32.

214 Aquinas, *Summa Theologiae* III:69:4 ad 2, emphasis added.

215 Ibid.

216 Ibid., III68:2 ad 2, emphasis added.

217 See Ott, *Fundamentals of Catholic Dogma*, 334.

218 Aquinas, *Summa Theologiae* III:63:3.

219 Council of Trent, *Decree on the Sacraments*, "Touching on the Sacraments in General," can. 9, in *The Canons and Decrees of the Council of Trent*, 52.

220 Cyril of Jerusalem, *Catechetical Lectures* 5.6, in *S. Cyril of Jerusalem, S. Gregory Nazianzen*, 30, emphasis added.

221 Cyril of Jerusalem, *Procatechesis* 16, in *S. Cyril of Jerusalem, S. Gregory Nazianzen*, 5.

222 Ibid., 17.35, 132.

223 Ibid., 16.24, 121, emphasis added.

224 Ott, *Fundamentals of Catholic Dogma*, 334.

225 See ibid., 335.

226 Cyril of Jerusalem, *Procatechesis* 17 in *S. Cyril of Jerusalem, S. Gregory Nazianzen*, 5.

227 See Aquinas, *Summa Theologiae* III:63:5.

228 Ibid., III:63:3.

229 Ibid., ad 3.

230 Ibid., ad 2.

231 Ibid., ad 3.

232 See ibid., III:66:2. Cf. Peter Lombard, *Sentences*, bk. IV, chap. 3, art. 5.

233 See *Catechism of the Council of Trent*, pt. II, chap. 2, qu. 20.

234 Representative of this view were Peter Abelard and Bernard of Clairvaux. See Ott, *Fundamentals of Catholic Dogma*, 351.

235 Representative of this view was Hugo of St. Victor. See ibid.

236 See Ott, *Fundamentals of Catholic Dogma*, 351.

237 See ibid.

238 Ibid., 351-352.